SAN FRANCISCO
BAY AREA
SECOND EDITION

BILL & KEVIN McMILLON

THE MOUNTAINEERS BOOKS

Published by
The Mountaineers Books
1001 SW Klickitat Way, Suite 201
Seattle, WA 98134

Second edition, 2002; First edition of *Best Hikes with Children in San Francisco's North Bay*, 1992; First edition of *Best Hikes with Children in San Francisco's South Bay*, 1992.

Published simultaneously in Great Britain by Cordee, 3a DeMontfort Street, Leicester, England, LE1 7HD

Manufactured in the United States of America

Project Editor: Kathleen Cubley
Copy Editor: Karen Parkin
Series Cover and Book Design: The Mountaineers Books
Layout Artist: Jennifer LaRock Shontz
Mapmaker: Ben Pease

All photographs by the authors unless otherwise noted

Cover photograph © Bill McMillon
Frontispiece © Bill McMillon

Library of Congress Cataloging-in-Publication Data
McMillon, Bill, 1942–
    Best hikes with children in the San Francisco Bay Area / by Bill McMillon and Kevin McMillon.— 2nd ed.
        p. cm. — (Best hikes with children series)
    Rev. ed. of two books, both entitled: Best hikes with children. c1992.
    Includes index.
    ISBN 0-89886-786-X (pbk.)
    1. Hiking—California—San Francisco Bay Area—Guidebooks. 2. Outdoor recreation for children—California—San Francisco Bay Area—Guidebooks. 3. Family recreation—California—San Francisco Bay Area—Guidebooks. 4. San Francisco Bay Area (Calif.)—Guidebooks. I. McMillon, Kevin, 1982- II. Title. III. Best hikes with children.
GV199.42.C22 S26949 2001
917.94'60454—dc21
            2001007274

CONTENTS

SANTA CLARA COUNTY

SONOMA / MARIN COUNTIES

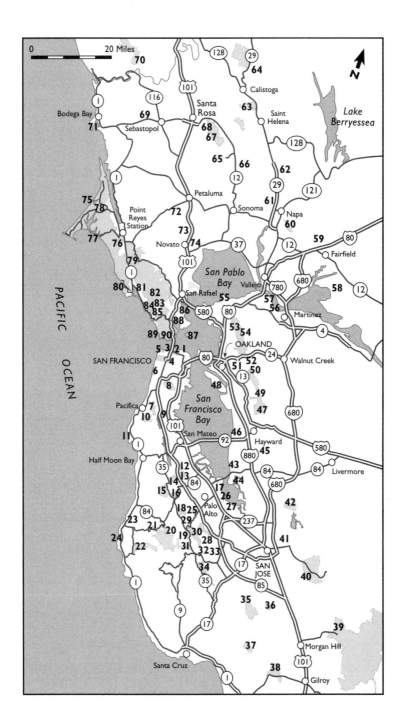

LEGEND

TRAILS

· · · · · · · · · · Featured Trail

= = = = = = Featured Fire Road or Jeep Trail
(no motor vehicles)

– · – · – · Featured Paved Trail or Path

· · · · · · · · · · · Other Trail

= = = = = = Other Fire Road or Jeep Trail
(no motor vehicles)

– · – · – · – Other Paved Trail or Path

ıııııııııııııı Stairs

ROADS

═══════ Freeway

━━━━━━ Major Road

────── Secondary Road

═══════ Unpaved Road

(80) Interstate

(101) US Highway

(128) (29) State Highway

SYMBOLS

(T) Trailhead

(P) Parking

→ Direction of Hike

⛺ Campground

🪑 Picnic Site

↔ Gate

⊔ Footbridge

River or Stream

Body of Water

Marsh

△ Summit or Peak

+—+—+—+ Railroad Right of Way

- - - - - - - - Power Line

—— · —— · Boundary Line

+++++++++ Fence

⊓ Bench

■ Building

● Point of Interest

○ Town

INTRODUCTION

Hiking with children is easy in the San Francisco Bay area. From small city and suburban parks to huge wilderness areas, you can find a challenging hike for any age any time of the year. Yes, any time, for the San Francisco Bay area is blessed with weather and parks that make for enjoyable hiking somewhere nearby in the midst of cold, rainy, foggy winters or during the hottest summer months.

My greatest pleasures in life have come from hiking along fog-shrouded ridges or through somber and solemn redwood forests of the San Francisco Bay area with my wife, children, and grandchildren for more than thirty years. And I am not alone in this pleasure, for thousands of Bay Area residents enjoy the many miles of wonderful trails that crisscross the ridges and canyons around San Francisco Bay. These lead along the tops of ridges that divide the peninsula to the south of San Francisco, across the oak-covered grasslands of the regional parks to the south and east of San Francisco, and through the redwood forests to the north. While there are no official numbers that I know of, there are several thousand miles of trails—perhaps as many as 4000—that lead not only

Take a break; enjoy the view

through developed parks near the region's population centers but also into vast wilderness areas where few hikers interfere with your enjoyment of nature.

The residents of the San Francisco Bay area are fortunate to have easy access to so much land that is protected from development. Many cities around the bay have set aside large parks where families can go for an afternoon hike. County parks, regional open space districts, and other agencies also have areas that offer hiking opportunities for the whole family.

The hikes in the guidebook represent just a sample of the many hikes available in the San Francisco Bay area. The hikes offer everyone—young and old—the chance to escape the hustle and bustle of city life. Some of the trails are heavily used, especially on summer weekends, but many are so lightly used that you may not encounter another hiker on a 5-mile hike through canyons or along open ridges. As you begin to explore, you will discover nearby trails that you will soon want to add to your own list of favorite hikes, especially in such areas as the Marin Headlands portion of the Golden Gate National Recreation Area and Point Reyes National Seashore, where hundreds of trails provide an almost unimaginable choice of family hikes.

In this revision of two books that Kevin and I wrote a decade ago, we have included trails from dense redwood forests to open seaside cliffs and high ridges that you can explore with your family, from young children to grandparents. Some are short, half-mile hikes suitable for even the youngest and oldest, while others are more than 5 miles long for those who want to both enjoy nature and engage in vigorous physical activity. These give you a great start on your explorations of the region.

HIKING WITH CHILDREN

Some children can't resist stopping to wade along a slow-moving stream, or watch an acorn woodpecker drill holes in a pine tree. Others want to push on up a trail to reach a hidden beach or an exposed mountain peak as quickly as possible. Each enjoys hikes in his or her special way, and does so with great bursts of enthusiasm. And parents find such eagerness contagious.

Even the most enthusiastic child sometimes needs a little encouragement to make it through a day's hike, however, and the following guidelines can help you get through those times—making hikes fun for all.

Know Your Family's Preferences

Each family has its own ideas about hiking. While some decide on a destination and concentrate on reaching it, others are more spontaneous, and reaching a particular destination is of only secondary importance. The same is true for members of a family: some like to surge ahead along the trail to a rest stop where they may dawdle for a while; others like to take a more leisurely pace along the trail with shorter rest stops.

After an outing or two you will know what your family prefers, and you can plan future trips with those preferences in mind.

Plan a Destination

Talk about your destination before you begin hiking and tell everyone what there is to be seen and explored along the way. Find a creek, a particularly interesting tree, or an outstanding vista, and plan to stop there. You may not make all the planned stops, but your family will have markers to help measure their progress during the hike.

You don't need to be intimately familiar with a trail to do this; find information in this guide, or from other sources, to help plan a hike.

A long walk down a natural tunnel

Plan for Nourishment and Rest

Always carry plenty of water or other liquids, and snacks, even on short hikes. Use these as incentives when your charges begin dragging, the trail gets steep, or the day gets warm. To encourage them to continue along the trail, remind tired children that you will stop at the next shady spot to drink some water and nibble "energy food." Also, remember to take plenty of "energy" stops so no one on the hike gets overly tired.

"Adopt" a Child for the Day

You may want to bring a friend or friends along on the hike so each child has a companion with whom to share discoveries.

Accentuate the Positive

Praise such as "you certainly did a good job coming up that hill" is important to children, and it lets them know that you appreciate how much effort they are putting into an activity.

If a child shows signs of slowing down on a difficult section of a trail, use patience and distractions to coax them along. Try casually observing some trailside plants or rocks as your child overtakes you, or say "look at that soaring hawk."

Encourage Tired Children

While most parents have a good idea of how far their children can hike and plan their outings with those limitations in mind, sometimes the best-laid plans go awry. Use your creativity and rely on a contigency "turnaround" plan to overcome what may seem like an insurmountable problem.

Here's one example of how our family turned a potentially disastrous hiking experience into a positive one. In the mid-1970s my wife and I took our four-year-old son on a camping trip to Point Reyes National Seashore with a group of high school students. All went well until the last day of the trip, when we discovered that we had neglected to thoroughly study a topographical map of the area. The first portion of the trail from Wildcat Canyon to Bear Valley was a rugged climb, one that no four-year-old could make without help.

Even with the assistance of several teenagers who carried one of our packs and most of our supplies, we began the day with trepidation. The first haft-hour went fine, but drastic measures were soon needed. First, Mary and I used our snack supply and took turns heading up the trail to hide a goody behind a rock or a plant. We then encouraged Matt to scurry up the trail to find the treats. We followed each successful search with a short energy break so Matt could eat his snack.

This game got us over the hump, literally, and we made it to our car in a reasonable time. We learned a valuable lesson, however, and ever since we choose hikes that take in the abilities of everyone in the family, checking out the entire trail on a topographic map if we haven't hiked it before.

Of the many ways to avoid such problems on day hikes, the best is to develop contingency plans for turning back short of your original destination. To help with your hike plans, this guidebook includes "turnaround" sites for longer one-way hikes and the "point-of-no-return" for longer loop hikes where it will be shorter to continue than to go back.

Have Fun Along the Way

Hikes should be fun. Enjoy yourself and help others enjoy themselves. Explore the area along the trail, and experience the sights, sounds, and smells of nature as you move along the trail. Remember, your goal isn't necessarily to reach a specific destination but to enjoy an outing with your family and help your children enjoy and respect their natural environment.

KNOWING TRAIL ETIQUETTE

Regardless of how well you plan a hike, or how well behaved your children are, sometimes things go wrong. Even during these times, all hikers—adults and children alike—must follow certain rules of behavior.

Some get to take in the view while the rest catch up

The Call of Nature

All the suggestions of "go to the bathroom now, there isn't one on the trail" won't prevent an occasional crisis when your child has to go, and immediately. If the child merely has to urinate, take him or her at least 200 feet from any trail or creek. If your child must defecate, dig a hole at least six inches deep in which to bury the feces. Wrap the used toilet paper (you should always carry a small roll) in a plastic bag and carry it out for disposal.

Uncontrolled Children

Hiking should be fun, but loud, uncontrolled children who run rapidly around blind trail curves and destroy plants and wildlife aren't fun for anyone. Always set ground rules for your children and their friends.

Talk about these rules well beforehand to help everyone develop a positive approach toward how to act in the wilderness. Rather than just talking about what not to do, help your children see what others do that is undesirable, and emphasize that "good hikers" don't do those things. By the time you get on the trail, they will be on the lookout for such negative behavior and will need little encouragement to avoid it themselves.

Another way children frequently violate trail etiquette is by cutting across switchbacks. Children love to slip and slide down a hill as they run ahead of others, but the practice is devastating to the hillsides, and often leads to washed-out trails. Remind them of the damage this causes and point out a few examples along the trail to make your case.

Family Pets

Don't bring them, even if the rules of the trail say you can. Although Rover may like outings as much as other members of the family, most trails just aren't appropriate for pets, especially if you want to enjoy the plants and animals along the way.

Fires

Do not build fires in any of the parks mentioned here except in designated sites at campgrounds and picnic areas. This is vitally important, because most of the trails in this guide are in or near habitats that become extremely volatile during the hot, dry months between May and October. Many parks even prohibit smoking during dry summer months.

Trail Right-of-Way

While hikers have as much right to use the trails as any other group, out of simple courtesy and a sense of safety they should give the right-of-way to mountain bikers and horseback riders. When you hear them coming, step off the trail, wait for them to pass, and avoid making any loud noises or sudden movement as they pass.

Leave Nothing but Footprints—Take Nothing but Photos

The hikes in this guide are in regional, state, or national parks, all of which have rules about collecting and against destroying plants, animals, and other natural items. Help your children understand these rules, and why they exist. If you don't know the park rules, contact the local rangers for information.

Use this opportunity to develop a wilderness ethic for your family by emphasizing how parks have been set aside for all to enjoy. Littering and destroying plants and animals (even collecting often results in heedless destruction) defeat that purpose.

ENJOYING NATURE

While hiking can be an end unto itself, most children like to investigate the ins and outs of the world around them, and that includes sites along trails. A creek becomes something more than just a body of water to cross. It becomes a place to investigate: where smooth, round rocks can be skipped across large pools; where insect larvae can be discovered under slimy bottom rocks; where frogs can be found in creekside vegetation; and where feet can be soaked as energy food is consumed. Trees, boulders, and hillsides provide the same attraction. So use their natural curiosity to introduce the study of nature, and do this in a sharing way.

Acorn woodpeckers have been busy on this fir tree.

Share, Don't Teach

As you walk along the trail and stop to rest, let your children share in your interests. Point out a pretty wildflower. If your child is interested, discuss where the flower grows, what insects are around it, and other observations. (You can do all of these without ever knowing the flower's name).

While hiking, you don't have to teach children anything. They can experience it right along with you. And you can experience anew the delight of investigating a creek bed, a tree, or a bluff through their eyes.

Use All Your Senses

Watch the light fall across a meadow, smell a pine tree, and touch a thistle. Even taste a limestone rock. Use all of your senses to experience nature.

Get the Feel of Nature

When your child complains about the trail being hot and dusty, ask how the animals in the area cope with the midday heat, and where they find refreshments. Suggest that the shade of the forest ahead may bring about a change in mood, and offer a drink or snack to help refresh the body as well as the spirit. Once you reach the shady forest, discuss how the animals that live nearby might enjoy similar breaks during their day.

Relating moods and experiences to the native wildlife helps you and your children become more in touch with the natural world and adds immeasurably to your hiking experience.

With these suggestions, and thoughts of your own, you will find trails in this guide that will give you many hours of pleasant outdoor activity. Go and enjoy, but be sure to make some preparations before you set out.

GETTING READY FOR DAY HIKES

Although it is possible to simply hop in your car and drive to a hiking trail with no preparation, it is not necessarily wise. A little preparation makes all hikes more enjoyable and may prevent unnecessary trouble.

The Ten Essentials

The Mountaineers recommends carrying these ten items on every hike, whether a day trip or an overnight. When you plan to bring children and want to make the trip as trouble-free as possible, these "Ten Essentials" may help you avert disaster.

1. **Extra clothing.** It may rain, the temperature may drop, or wading may be too tempting to pass up. Be sure to include rain gear, extra shoes and socks (especially a pair of shoes that can be used for wading), a warm sweater, and a hat and light gloves.
2. **Extra food.** Extra high-energy snacks are essential for active children and adults. Carry sufficient water in canteens and fanny packs in case no suitable source is available on the trail.
3. **Sunglasses.** Look for a pair that screens out UV rays.
4. **Knife.** Chances are you will never need it, but bring one along anyway. A knife with multiple blades, scissors, tweezers, and a bottle opener is handy.
5. **Fire starter**—candle or chemical fuel. If you must build a fire, these are indispensable.
6. **First-aid kit.** Don't forget to include moleskin for blisters, baking soda to apply to stings, extra sunscreen, and any special medication your child might need, for example if he or she is allergic to bee stings or other insect bites.
7. **Matches in a waterproof container.** You can buy these matches in a store that carries hiking and camping gear.
8. **Flashlight.** Check the batteries before you leave home.
9. **Map.** Don't assume you'll just "feel" your way to the summit. Maps are important, and I discuss them more below.
10. **Compass.** Teach your children how to use it, too.

In addition to these ten essentials, the following suggestions will help make hikes more enjoyable.

What to Wear

You won't need special clothes or shoes for day hiking in the San Francisco Bay area. The generally well-marked and stable trails don't demand heavy-duty hiking boots, and specialty clothing is unneccesary because of the Bay Area's equable climate.

Children can wear the active-wear shoes that they usually put on for school and play. Sneakers, especially high tops, give adequate support and are usually well broken in. This helps keep blisters to a minimum, thereby avoiding one of the most uncomfortable aspects of hiking.

To enjoy hiking in the San Francisco Bay area, you should wear layers that can be removed and put back on as the day's weather changes from windy and foggy to sunny and warm, and back again. Because hiking is a year-round activity in the Bay Area, and there are so many microclimates throughout the region, it is difficult to say exactly what clothing you should carry on any one hike. Rain gear is generally important only in the winter, with an occasional storm in the fall or spring, but a hat or a cap is useful year-round to protect adults and children alike from the effects of the sun.

Packs

Not everyone needs to carry a pack on a day hike, but children usually love to carry their own to hold their special items. Adults' daypacks should be large enough to carry bulky clothing and extra food and drinks, but youngsters can use either day or fanny packs. Adult packs should accommodate food, small items such as magnifying glasses, individual drinking containers, layers of clothing that may be removed along the way, and the Ten Essentials.

Other Items

Although they are not essential, some small items are fun to bring along to encourage children to explore the world of nature close-up and to give them something to do during rest and eating breaks. Consider packing the following: lightweight binoculars (one pair per family should do, but some families have several) for looking at birds and animals, as well as scouting the trail ahead; a magnifying glass and insect boxes for short-term viewing of small animals and plants; a lightweight camera for recording the trip; and possibly some nature guides to help identify objects in the field. You can use your knife to dig around in old stumps and under rocks when searching for creepy crawlers.

Maps

Because these trails are in developed parks, you are unlikely to get lost on any of these hikes, although some of the longer ones do take you away from the most heavily traveled areas of the larger parks. However, a little common sense, a copy of the park brochure, and an awareness of where the trail is should keep you on track.

Most hiking and camping stores in the Bay Area sell topographic maps, compasses, and instruction books on how to use these tools. These aren't strictly necessary, but can be a fun and interesting way for children to determine how to find your exact position on the trail.

Food and Drinks

Outings are a good time to let your children indulge in a few high-energy foods such as candy bars and other sweet snacks as treats. Use these as motivation to get to that shady tree up the trail where you can stop for a rest, or over the hump to the top of a ridge. Also take along fruit and high-protein food children like for lunch breaks.

Children like to carry some food in their own packs, but you can hold back special treats until they are needed for motivation. Remember: one of the Ten Essentials is extra food. Whatever you take on the hike, don't skimp. It is always better to carry extra food home than to have hikers become cranky and disagreeable from hunger.

Another item that you absolutely must not skimp on is fluids. Many of the hikes in this guide can be hot and dry during the summer months, and few have drinking water available.

While sugary and sports drinks are fine for replacing lost fluids, never depend solely upon them. On Kevin's sixth birthday we took a group of boys on a hike to Lake Ilsanjo in Annadel State Park, and took along only snack drinks to have with lunch and along the trail. The June day was hot, there was no potable water at the lake, and several of the boys complained loudly about their need for "real" water during the 5-mile round trip to the lake and back.

First Aid and Safety

Many hiking books place a big emphasis on first aid and safety, but in reality I have found that my children have less need for first aid on the trail than during a normal day at home.

Nevertheless, my "Ten Essentials" first-aid kit includes the following: large and small Band Aids, antibacterial cream, a squeeze bottle of hydrogen peroxide, a patch of moleskin, scissors, an athletic bandage, medicine for relief of insect stings, and some itch medicine. Recently I have also begun carrying a cold wrap, but I must admit this is more for me than for my children.

Also, be sure to carry sunscreen and insect repellent. While biting insects aren't a major problem in the Bay Area, there are times when mosquitoes and flies can be bothersome, and the repellent helps. Sunscreen is an absolute necessity, especially for those of us so fair-skinned as to "burn while on the back side of the moon," because many trails cover long distances where there is little or no shade.

In addition to active childrens' normal scrapes and falls, nature also offers several dangers and worries that parents must watch for and caution children about.

Poison Oak, Nettles, and Thistles. Know what these plants look like during various seasons, as skin exposure to any of these plants can cause either an immediate or a delayed reaction, which is often uncomfortable.

Stinging nettles cause a more immediate reaction than poison oak (which generally doesn't appear for two days to two weeks after exposure) and can be quite painful—even excruciatingly so—to children and adults alike. Various types of thistles also cause intense pain and itching for some people.

Itch medicines help with, but don't completely relieve, the discomfort of stinging nettles. The best solution is to avoid contact. If you don't know what the various plants look like, park rangers will be glad to help you identify them, and many parks have signs illustrating poison oak and nettles. If you are hiking in areas such as Point Reyes, where nettles and thistles are abundant, you may want to take along a guidebook that can help you identify them.

Even the prickly plants add beauty and interest to a hike.

Stinging Insects. Some parks in this guide have large numbers of stinging insects such as yellow jackets, which can be *scary* to children. While their stings are painful, they don't have to be cause for ending a hike. Bring along an over-the-counter medicine that relieves the discomfort when rubbed on a sting.

Rattlesnakes. Many parks in this guide have large populations of rattlers that come out during warm spring and hot summer months. Very few hikers ever see these reclusive animals, but take a few simple precautions to avoid a bite: Never stick your hand down into rocky crevices without first looking. Never climb rock faces where you have to put your hands into holes for handholds. Always watch where you are stepping when you step over logs and rocks.

Rattlesnakes are poisonous, and they do occasionally bite people, but their bites are seldom fatal. If, by chance, a rattlesnake bites a member of your hiking party, don't panic. Have the person who was bitten lie down and remain still, and send another member of the group to find a ranger or a phone. Let the authorities, whether a ranger or 911, know where the victim is located, and when the bite occurred. With modern medicine, there is little danger if medical attention is given promptly.

Lost and Injured Children. Bay Area trails are generally safe, but parents must diligently protect their children from two potential dangers: falling from rocks and cliffs and getting lost.

Children love to climb on rocks and cliffs, and have great fun doing so, but the crumbly sandstone cliffs that are so common along the Bay Area shoreline are the most dangerous that can be found. No child or adult should climb on them because they present definite and immediate danger. Even walking too close to the edges of these cliffs places hikers in danger.

Also, children love to explore, sometimes straying from the group and becoming lost and panic-stricken. Search-and-rescue units spend many hours searching for lost children in the parks of the region, and members often speak to school and youth groups about how to avoid this lonely and terrifying experience. First, they advise that everyone carry a loud whistle. Second, they recommend that anyone separated from the group, and unable to gain attention with a whistle, "hug" a tree (or a bush or boulder). This means the child should sit down next to a tree, or bush, or boulder, and stay there until found. The only other action the lost person should take is to blow a whistle or shout loudly at regular intervals.

UNDERSTANDING THE NATURAL HISTORY OF THE SAN FRANCISCO BAY AREA

In the San Francisco Bay area you will find a wide variety of plant and animal communities, including some—such as the coast redwood forests—that grow only in Northern California. Although many hikers enjoy their outings without ever learning anything about either the plants or the animals that they may encounter, I enjoy my outings more when I learn something about various natural communities and how the plants and animals interact with one another. Both the University of California Press and Wilderness Press publish a number of useful natural history guidebooks. Here are a few examples of the flora and fauna you most likely will see in your wanderings.

Chaparral

Many California hills are covered by a dense growth of hard-leafed, drought-resistant plants collectively known as chaparral. The plants in this community are well adapted to the long, dry summers and wet winters of Northern California, for they tolerate the hot dry spells and protect the hillsides during the wet winter months. In addition, they regenerate quickly from fires.

The plants in these communities include various species of manzanita, which has shiny red bark on its trunk and branches and ranges from low creepers to 15-foot-tall shrubs; ceanothus, sometimes called California lilac, with its large clusters of blue or white flowers; and chamise, a member of the rose family that spreads into almost impenetrable thickets that are 2 to 10 feet high.

Coastal Scrub

The plants in these communities are softer than most chaparral, and the dominant plant is coyote brush. Coastal scrub is found near the ocean and bay, where there is more moisture and less heat.

Wildflowers

Wildflowers such as California poppy and blue lupine are familiar to everyone who has driven along the highways of Northern California, but there are dozens more native wildflowers that can be identified along the trails in this guide.

Sometimes you have to get on your knees to appreciate small beauties.

Trees

Several species of trees are so common in the region that you will probably encounter at least one species on almost every hike in this book. These include the many species of oak that are native to the region (and it is hard for some people to distinguish between these); various species of exotic eucalyptus (brought here from Australia in the nineteenth century); bay, which is also known as California laurel, pepperwood, and myrtle; buckeye, a member of the horse-chestnut family; madrone, with its distinctive smooth red trunk and peeling bark; Douglas-fir, an important lumber tree that grows to a height of 300 feet; and the coast redwood, the tallest tree in the world.

Mammals

Along the trail you may encounter or observe signs of raccoon, opossum, gray squirrel, chipmunk, ground squirrel, rabbit, coyote, gray fox, bobcat, and black-tailed deer. In some parks you may even see signs of bear and cougar, but you're not likely to run into either.

None of these present any danger to hikers, with the possible exception of bear and cougar (and there have been no reports of attacks by either in the Bay Area in many years), and children delight in seeing animals in their natural habitat.

You may spot sea lions and harbor seals in and around the bay and ocean.

Always keep an eye out for potential dangers.

Even fog can't keep the view from being captivating.

Birds

You will run across various hawks, vultures, jays, and a number of types of gulls, which are all common in the region. A bird guide will help you identify the many smaller birds that you will encounter on your hikes.

USING THIS GUIDE

The hikes in this guide are located in the Bay Area counties of San Francisco, San Mateo, Santa Clara, Alameda, Contra Costa, Solano, Napa, Sonoma, and Marin, and are located within county, regional, state, and federal parks and reserves. Most parks provide maps or brochures that describe the trails within their boundaries and tell something about the natural history of the region. You can obtain these either at the parks or from park district offices. Addresses and phone numbers of park district headquarters are listed at the end of this introduction.

Although the trails in the guide are permanent, at times park officials temporarily close or reroute trails because of landslide, fire danger, or other natural conditions. You can call the park where you intend to hike to ask about the latest trail conditions and find out if the trail you intend to use is open. If it isn't, you can ask about similar trails nearby, and most park officials will gladly help.

The hikes in this guide represent just a small percentage of the total miles of trails available in the nine counties. More than 1000 miles of trails cover the East Bay Regional Parks alone, which is just one of several large park systems in the region.

We narrowed our selection to just ninety hikes (a difficult task) with the following criteria in mind. First, some of the hikes must be enjoyable to everyone—toddlers and seniors alike. Second, the majority of hikes must be moderate enough for most families to derive a sense of accomplishment after completing them. Third, some hikes must be difficult enough to challenge older children (up to twelve years old) in good physical condition who like to hike. Fourth, the hikes must expose hikers to the wide range of natural habitats that exist in the Bay Area. Open grasslands, oak woodlands, mixed oak and madrone forests, mixed conifer forests, redwood and fir forests, tidelands, and seashore are all represented.

Each hike entry begins with quick information about length, difficulty, and location, and tells something about the natural history of the region covered by the trails.

One last thought. This is a guide to day hikes in the Bay Area, but several of the park systems in the region have developed environmental and hike-in campsites where you can backpack for one or more nights. After you have explored many of the trails and decided you want a more adventurous family outing, consider one of these overnight backpacks.

PARK DISTRICT HEADQUARTERS

The following is a listing of the district headquarters of the local, county, regional, state, and national parks where the hikes in this guide are located. If you have any questions about the conditions of the trails—whether it is too wet or hot or dry to hike in the park, what wildflowers are blooming, etc.—give them a call. They are always willing to answer questions or refer you to someone who can.

Angel Island State Park
P.O. Box 318
Tiburon, CA 94920
415-435-1915

Annadel State Park
6201 Channel Drive
Santa Rosa, CA 95405
707-539-3911

California State Parks
P.O. Box 9
Pescadero, CA 94060
408-879-0173

East Bay Municipal Utility District
500 San Pablo Dam Road
Orinda, CA 94563
925-254-3778

East Bay Regional Park District
2950 Peralta Oaks Court
P.O. Box 5381
Oakland, CA 94605-0381
510-635-0135

Golden Gate National Recreation Area
Fort Mason, Building 201
San Francisco, CA 94123
415-556-0560

Henry W. Coe State Park
P.O. Box 846
Morgan Hill, CA 95038
408-779-2728

Marin County Open Space District
Marin County Civic Center
San Rafael, CA 94903
415-499-6387

Midpeninsula Regional Open Space District
330 Distel Circle
Los Altos, CA 94022
650-691-1200

San Francisco Bay National Wildlife Refuge
1 Marshland Road
Fremont, CA 94536
510-792-0222

San Francisco Recreation and Park Department
McLaren Lodge, Golden Gate Park
501 Stanyan Street
San Francisco, CA 94117
415-666-7200

San Mateo County Parks and Recreation
590 Hamilton Street
Redwood City, CA 94063
415-363-4020

Santa Clara County Parks and Recreation Department
298 Garden Hill Drive
Los Gatos, CA 95030
408-358-3741

Solano County Farmlands and Open Space Foundation
P.O. Box 115
Fairfield, CA 94533
707-428-7580

Sonoma County Parks Department
2300 County Center Drive
Santa Rosa, CA 95403
707-527-2041

Although not part of the park system, several Bay Area trail and hiking organizations provide current information on trails and hikes. These include:

California Trails and Greenways Foundation
P.O. Box 183
Los Altos, CA 94023
415-948-1829

Santa Cruz Mountains Trail Association
P.O. Box 1141
Los Altos, CA 94023
415-948-9098

The Trail Center
4898 El Camino Real
Office 205 A
Los Altos, CA 94022
415-968-7065

KEY TO SYMBOLS

 Day hikes. These are hikes that can be completed in a single day. While some trips allow camping, only a few require it.

 Easy trails. These are relatively short, smooth, gentle trails suitable for small children or first-time hikers.

 Moderate trails. Most of these are 2 to 4 miles total distance and feature more than 500 feet of elevation gain. The trail may be rough and uneven. Hikers should wear lug-soled boots and be sure to carry the Ten Essentials.

 Difficult trails. These are often rough, with considerable elevation gain or distance to travel. They are suitable for older or experienced children. Lug-soled boots and the Ten Essentials are standard equipment.

 Hikable. The best times of year to hike each trail are indicated by the following symbols: flower—spring; sun—summer; leaf—fall; snowflake—winter.

 Driving directions. These paragraphs tell you how to get to the trailheads.

 Turnarounds. These are places, mostly along moderate trails, where families can cut their hike short yet still have a satisfying outing. Turnarounds usually offer picnic opportunities, views, or special natural attractions.

 Cautions. These mark potential hazards—cliffs, stream or highway crossings, and the like—where close supervision of children is strongly recommended.

 Environmental close-ups. These highlight special environmental elements along the trail and help children learn about nature and learn to respect nature.

A NOTE ABOUT SAFETY

Safety is an important concern for all outdoor activities. No guidebook can alert you to every hazard or anticipate the limitations of every reader. Therefore, the descriptions of roads, trails, routes, and natural features in this book are not representations that a particular place or excursion will be safe for your party. When you follow any of the routes described in this book, you assume responsibility for your own safety. Under normal conditions, such excursions require the usual attention to traffic, road and trail conditions, weather, terrain, the capabilities of your party, and other factors. Keeping informed on current conditions and exercising common sense are the keys to a safe, enjoyable outing.

The Mountaineers Books

Look closely for small spots of color.

ACKNOWLEDGMENTS

In the first edition of this book I noted that my nine-year-old son, Kevin, was listed as co-author for a very good reason. Without his interest in hiking and nature, it may very well have never been written. As a companion on the trail, and as a constant push at home (especially when he attempted to compute what his share of the income from the book would be), Kevin played an important role from start to finish. Now 19 years old, Kevin has become an even more active participant in revising this guidebook. He photographed many of the images that appear in these pages and re-hiked many of the trails to note any significant changes made to them during the past decade.

My wife, Mary, also still deserves mention, for she has now been a trail companion for more than thirty years, and has even changed so that she no longer prefers what she describes as "Midwest walks" where there are few hills.

Finally, I wish to thank the people at The Mountaineers Books for giving me the opportunity to share some of my favorite hikes with others.

Bill McMillon

SAN FRANCISCO/
SAN MATEO COUNTIES

1

CRISSY FIELD-FORT POINT TRAIL

Type ▪	Day hike
Difficulty ▪	Moderate for children
Distance ▪	1.5 miles, one way
Hiking time ▪	2 hours
Elevation gain ▪	Level
Hikable ▪	Year-round
Map ▪	Golden Gate National Recreation Area Park Guide

Crissy Field is located along the southern shoreline of San Francisco Bay between the Palace of Fine Arts, with its wonderful Exploratorium, and Fort Point, an old Civil War–era fort that sits beneath the southern tower of the Golden Gate Bridge.

For years the area was the industrial backwater of the Presidio, with run-down buildings and toxic dumps alongside the old Army airfield. Between 1998 and 2001 this area was transformed from an eyesore with little public use into a showpiece, complete with a recreated tidal marsh that mimics a natural system where the tidal ebb and flow continually changes the surrounding tidal marsh and dunes ecosystem. This natural evolution of the system concerns those, such as windsurfers, who wish to see a static system where the placement of dunes and sandbars do not move. Nevertheless, it

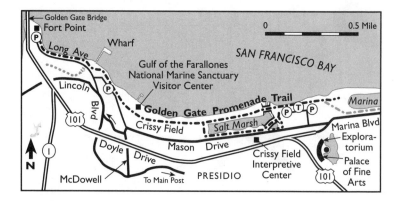

Tidal marsh with a view

sustains a rich community of plants and animals, including many shorebirds that once again stop over in the marsh area on their long migrations between the Arctic and South America.

To reach this hike, enter Crissy Field from Marina Drive. You cannot make a left turn off Doyle Drive where it becomes Marina Drive, so you must drive east along Marina to the park entrance. After entering the park, take the first left to the parking lot along the beach.

From the parking lot walk west along the trail to the restored marsh and continue over the bridge that crosses it. Go through the gate onto the bridge and have everyone keep an eye out for the wide variety of birds that generally congregate in the water and along its edges. The plants that cover the dunes here are all natives that have been re-introduced since the marsh has been restored.

After about 0.25 mile the bridge ends at the sidewalk that runs along Mason Drive; you can see the Crissy Field Interpretive Center across the street to your right. Now is a good time to make a visit so everyone can learn more about the restoration project and the many activities that occur in the Golden Gate National Recreation Area.

Return to the sidewalk and continue west for another 0.25 mile to where the trail heads toward the beach over what remains of the old Crissy Airfield, which was constructed in 1919 for the Army Air Corps. This trail rejoins the Golden Gate Promenade Trail that extends from the parking lot to Fort Point.

All along this stretch of trail, as well as along the section you bypassed when you crossed the marsh bridge, there is beach access where the children can play in the sand and water.

At about 1 mile you pass by the Gulf of the Farallones National Marine Sanctuary Visitor Center. There you can learn more about the marine residents of the region, from the large marine mammals that frequent both the bay and the open ocean outside the Golden Gate to the many seabirds that live nearby year-round, as well as those that migrate along the coast each fall and spring.

Continue along the trail to Fort Point, a restored Civil War fortress that was never used for battle, but where the children can enjoy acting out military fantasies.

Return to the parking lot by the promenade, stopping by the beaches that you bypassed on the way to the fort.

2 PRESIDIO ECOLOGY TRAIL LOOP

Type ■	Day hike
Difficulty ■	Moderate for children
Distance ■	2-mile loop
Hiking time ■	2 hours
Elevation gain ■	200 feet
Hikable ■	Year-round
Map ■	Golden Gate National Recreation Area Park Guide

Soldiers have staffed the Presidio since the first Spanish garrison arrived there in 1776, making it the oldest continuously used military post in the United States. The Presidio Army Museum, located at the corner of Lincoln Boulevard and Funston Street, documents the 200-plus years of military occupation of this beautiful corner of San Francisco. Early soldiers at the Presidio complained of the harsh environment of the sand dunes where the fort was located, and the Army Corps of Engineers developed a plan to landscape the area with non-native trees in 1883. More than 60,000 trees were planted in the area during the 1880s alone. Today's visitors can see at least 30 different types of trees along the Ecology Trail Loop and many more—including acacia, cypress, eucalyptus, madrone, redwood, spruce, and Portuguese cork oak—throughout the Presidio.

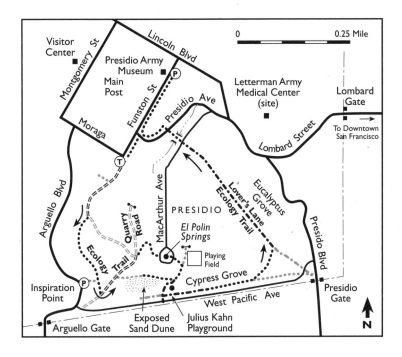

Enter the Presidio at the Lombard Street Gate and curve around the Letterman Army Medical Center on Lombard until it dead-ends at Lincoln Boulevard. Take a left on Lincoln and go one block to Funston Street. Turn left on Funston and left again into the parking lot across the street from the museum.

To reach the trailhead for the Ecology Trail Loop, head southwest along Funston Street for about 0.25 mile, where Funston dead-ends. The trail begins straight ahead as a fire road.

The trail winds along the side of a hill and goes through a forest of eucalyptus, Monterey pine, and other exotic trees that were planted to help retain the sand dunes and break the monotony of the barren land that the Presidio was built on. Ask your children to count how many different kinds of trees and shrubs they can distinguish and to discuss why the Army planted them.

At about 0.5 mile from the parking area a trail heads off to the right, but veer to the left and continue around the hillside. After another 200 yards a narrow trail leads downhill to the left. Continue straight ahead on the road.

A grassy meadow opens up on the hillside above the trail at about

0.75 mile, and the views of the forest below make this a pleasant place to rest.

Several hundred yards past the hillside meadows, the trail dead-ends into another fire road. Take a right here.

Housing is visible downhill from the trail as it veers to the right around the hill. At about 1 mile a small park can be seen downhill on the left, and a small, lightly used trail leads down to it. You may take the trail down to the park for a rest at the picnic site near the historic site of El Polin Springs. The springs were the primary source of water for the early Spanish soldiers at the Presidio, and were used for many years. You can talk about the history of the Presidio as you take a break, or you can head up the steps to the south side of the Julius Kahn Playground picnic site, where there are slides and other play equipment.

You can also reach the playground by continuing along the main trail. It passes through a section of exposed sand dunes just a few hundred feet before the playground, and then becomes a paved walkway.

The walkway continues past the playground beside West Pacific Avenue and leads through a cypress grove. At about 1.25 miles an easily missed trail leads off to the left. This trail takes you to the paved Lover's Lane, but if you miss it and end up at Presidio Boulevard, simply turn left for about 100 feet along Presidio until you come to the signs for Lover's Lane.

Keep an eye out for small wonders on the tips of limbs.

Take a left there, and head downhill to MacArthur Avenue. A large eucalyptus grove is uphill from the lane and a housing unit is downhill.

Lover's Lane crosses MacArthur Avenue at about 1.75 miles. A creek divides a small meadow between MacArthur and Presidio. Cross the meadow; the small, brick footbridge; and Presidio Boulevard before turning left.

Continue up Presidio for about 100 yards until you reach Funston. Turn right on Funston, and return to the parking lot.

You may want to visit the museum, where the children can learn about the history of the Presidio.

3 FORT POINT–BAKER BEACH COAST TRAIL

Type ▪ Day hike
Difficulty ▪ Moderate to difficult for children
Distance ▪ 4 miles, round trip
Hiking time ▪ 3 hours
Elevation gain ▪ 300 feet gain and loss
Hikable ▪ Year-round
Map ▪ Golden Gate National Recreation Area Park Guide

The 2-mile stretch of oceanfront cliffs and beach between Fort Point beneath the Golden Gate Bridge and Baker Beach has a long military history. From the Gold Rush period before the Civil War until World War II, Fort Point and a number of bunkers and gun batteries were built to protect the San Francisco harbor from invasion by enemy forces. These fortifications were never used in war and slowly became obsolete as military strategy changed with the advent of nuclear weapons and ICBMs. The relics of these earlier eras remain for adults and children to explore, however, and serve as good rest stops on this hike between Fort Point and Baker Beach.

Follow the signs from the south of the Golden Gate Bridge toll plaza to the parking lot for Fort Point at the end of Marine Drive. The trail leads uphill toward the southern end of the bridge from the picnic area at Fort Point.

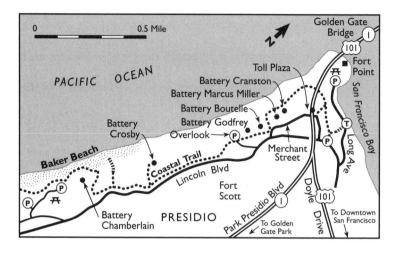

The trail ascends from Fort Point with a series of switchbacks along the bay side of the bridge. This continues for several hundred yards to a junction where one trail leads to an observation platform near the toll plaza, one to the left toward several bunkers, and one to the right under the bridge. Take the trail to the right and head along the top of the cliff. From here you can look back north to the Marin Headlands or south toward Lands End.

The trail leads along the edge of the cliff, and at about 0.5 mile Battery Cranston and Battery Marcus Miller can be seen to your left. You can explore these cleverly camouflaged fortifications now, or wait until you return. Your children will love to explore as many of these batteries as you let them, and sometimes they will get distracted from the hike. Emphasize that there are a number of batteries along the trail and that you will be returning on the same route.

The trail heads inland as you pass these batteries, and at about 0.75 mile comes to a parking lot adjacent to Merchant Drive. Battery Boutelle is located here, and is more accessible than the first two were.

A few hundred feet past Battery Boutelle the trail passes by Battery Godfrey, and comes to a small side road that leads to the Fort Scott Overlook. This overlook makes a good rest stop.

From the Fort Scott Overlook the trail again turns inland and is soon separated from Lincoln Boulevard by only a barrier. Caution your children of the dangers along this trail section: Poison oak grows along the trail here, and occasionally you may encounter heavy traffic.

Some days a person just feels like being alone.

At just past 1 mile a side trail leads down to Battery Crosby. This side trip is about 0.25 mile each way.

At about 1.25 miles another side trail leads down to Baker Beach over sand dunes. This area is being revegetated, so you should stay on the trail and not explore on the dunes. You can head down to the beach here or continue on the main trail to Battery Chamberlin at 1.5 miles. There are plans for this battery to be reconstructed so that visitors can see how the fortifications operated, but the lack of funds may delay the opening.

The trail reaches Baker Beach at 1.75 miles and continues to the end at 2 miles. Baker Beach has parking and picnic sites toward the southern end, and more than 1 mile of beach extending northward toward the Golden Gate.

Return to Fort Point along the same trail. One adult may stay with the children while the other returns to Fort Point if the return hike seems too difficult, or two cars can be used, one at each parking lot.

STOW LAKE TRAIL

Type ■	Day hike
Difficulty ■	Easy to moderate for younger children
Distance ■	1 mile
Hiking time ■	1 hour
Elevation gain ■	100-foot gain and loss
Hikable ■	Year-round
Map ■	Golden Gate Park

In 1870 the 1017 acres of what is now Golden Gate Park were mostly sand dunes, and far from the developed areas of the city to the east. Few people were in favor of expending the time and energy that were required to transform this bleak and little-visited area into a lush park, but time has proven them right. Today the park is an urban showpiece and one of San Francisco's most visited attractions.

Near the middle of this vast urban park is Stow Lake, an artificial lake complete with an artificial island, waterfall, and boulders.

To reach Stow Lake, follow the signs from either John F. Kennedy Drive to the north or Martin Luther King Jr. Drive to

Water birds find any pond in an urban environment.

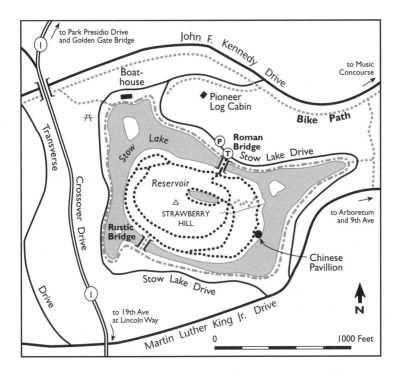

the south, just to the west of the California Academy of Sciences museum complex. Drive to the boathouse area on the road that circles the lake and continue east for several hundred yards to the Roman Bridge that crosses the lake to the island.

If you have very young children, take the level, 0.5-mile trail that follows along the edge of the lake around the island. To do this simply head to your right as you cross the Roman Bridge, keeping downhill at all trail splits. In fact, this is a good introduction to the hike for all children, for they get to see the many ducks and water birds that live in the lake, as well as the boats that people rent for water outings. The hike also gets everyone loosened up before they climb to the top of Strawberry Hill.

As you walk around the island, you pass by the Rustic Bridge, which is almost directly across the island from the Roman Bridge; a Chinese temple; and Huntington Falls, which runs out of a reservoir that sits near the top of the hill. Look closely at the many boulders along the trail, especially those at the falls. Close inspection reveals that these are really concrete replicas of real boulders that were constructed along with the rest of the island.

As you return to the Roman Bridge at 0.5 mile, you may want to take a short break and talk about the rest of the hike (if you have younger hikers), or you may simply head up the steps on your left. These take you up a steep slope for about 200 yards to a level spot where the reservoir for the falls is located. If the reservoir is full, you can follow the trail to your left as it takes you across a small bridge that sits at the top of the falls. Again, inspect the imitation boulders that make up the waterfall.

Return to the reservoir area and take the trail that heads around it. This takes you to a great picnic area on the top of the hill. After a rest and snack you can begin to head back downhill on any one of several trails. Let the children decide which trails to take, for they all lead back to the trail that circles the lake.

The total hike is about 1 mile.

5 **COASTAL TRAIL TO LANDS END**

Type ▪	Day hike
Difficulty ▪	Moderate for children
Distance ▪	1-mile loop
Hiking time ▪	2 hours
Elevation gain ▪	200 feet loss and gain
Hikable ▪	Year-round
Map ▪	Golden Gate National Recreation Area Park Guide

Lands End is the wildest, rockiest part of the coastline around San Francisco. The cliffs are unstable, and landslides frequently crash down during heavy storms. The area immediately off the point is just as dangerous, for many ships have run aground on the submerged rocks there. Wildflowers are profuse here in the spring.

 Park in the parking lot of the Palace of the Legion of Honor at the corner of E1 Camino Del Mar and Legion of Honor Drive. From the lot walk to E1 Camino Del Mar and turn left. The trailhead is about 200 yards ahead, at the end of E1 Camino Del Mar.

The trail almost immediately crosses a small footbridge and begins a gentle swing around the top of a small canyon. The trail crosses several small springs and creeks that feed the large creek in the canyon.

Head into the mist to find what's beyond.

Just before 0.25 mile the trail veers to the right and a fire road continues straight ahead. Take the trail to the right as it begins to head downhill in a series of steps. As it levels off at about 0.25 mile it dead-ends into the Coastal Trail. Turn right on the Coastal Trail, cross the large creek, and join another fire road about 100 yards past the creek.

A right turn here at the fire road takes you uphill to the golf course and the paved golf cart trail. Turn left instead, then go for about 50 yards on the fire road to a trail that leads off to the left. This trail heads

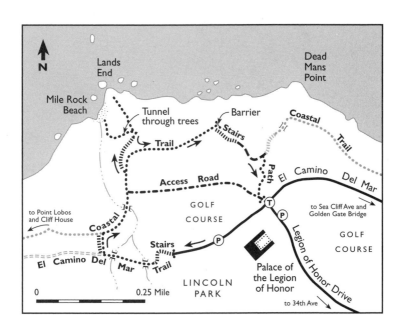

down to Lands End and passes through a ghostly forest of dead cypress trees. When fog shrouds the cliffs, the stark, gray snags can fill a child's imagination with many wonderful and *scary* images. At about 0.75 mile, just before the trail dead-ends at Lands End, another trail leads off toward Mile Rock Beach. You must travel through about 50 feet of tunnel formed by coastal scrub and cypress before you reach the top of the beach. The tunnel and beach are a good play area and rest stop that the children will enjoy.

As you return to the trail to Lands End, take the short trail out to the end; on a clear day the view is spectacular. On foggy days the sound of the surf far below adds to the eerie feeling of loneliness that often accompanies walks along the cliffs.

Return to the Coastal Trail, turn left, and continue to a barrier that blocks any further progress at about 0.9 mile. At that point a narrow trail leads up the side of the cliff back toward the golf course. About halfway up the steep wooden steps you will find a bench that offers a good view of the coastline on clear days.

Continue up the trail until it dead-ends at the paved golf cart trail. Turn left to return to the parking lot.

6 SUNSET TRAIL–FORT FUNSTON

Type ◼	Day hike
Difficulty ◼	Easy for children
Distance ◼	0.75-mile loop
Hiking time ◼	45 minutes
Elevation gain ◼	None
Hikable ◼	Year-round
Map ◼	Golden Gate National Recreation Area Park Guide

Fort Funston, with its great dunes, sandy bluffs, and steady ocean breezes, is one of the premier hang-gliding areas in the San Francisco Bay region. Wildflowers bloom profusely on the dunes and along the trails during the spring and early summer, and children love to explore Battery Davis, a 1938 casemated battery. It was the prototype for all sixteen-inch gun emplacements built in the United States after that.

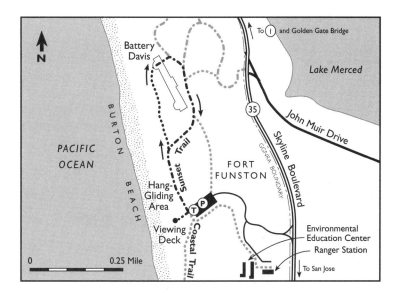

N

Battery Davis

PACIFIC
OCEAN

BURTON BEACH

Hang-Gliding Area

Sunset Trail

Viewing Deck

Coastal Trail

FORT FUNSTON

GGNRA BOUNDARY

Skyline Boulevard

To 1 and Golden Gate Bridge

Lake Merced

35

John Muir Drive

Environmental Education Center
Ranger Station

To San Jose

0   0.25 Mile

Drive south on the Great Highway (California Highway 1) until it becomes Skyline Boulevard at Lake Merced. Turn into the Fort Funston parking area about 0.5 mile past John Muir Drive, and continue to the rear of the parking area near the viewing deck.

Take the short walk to the viewing deck, where your children will like to observe the hang-gliding area and Burton Beach below. Return to the parking lot and head north on the Sunset Trail. This was the first wheelchair-accessible trail built along the California coast, and it is an easy trail for the whole family, even those with babies in strollers or grandparents in wheelchairs.

Benches and picnic tables are scattered along the side of the trail as it leads through open dunes and coastal scrub until it reaches

Explore a remnant of times past.

Battery Davis at just under 0.5 mile. Children like to explore this old fortification, and you may want to discuss why the batteries were built and the mood of the country during the 1930s.

The paved trail leads through the battery, encircles it, and returns to the parking lot at 0.75 mile.

Beware that this is one of the few off-leash trails around San Francisco. If you have small children, or older ones who are afraid of large dogs, tell them there will be dogs running free on the trail. You also must watch for piles of dog poop along the path.

7 SWEENEY RIDGE TRAIL TO SAN FRANCISCO BAY DISCOVERY SITE

Type ▪	Day hike
Difficulty ▪	Difficult for children
Distance ▪	4 miles round trip or loop with return via Sneath Lane
Hiking time ▪	3 hours
Elevation gain ▪	500 feet, plus loss and gain of 300 feet in ravine
Hikable ▪	Year-round
Map ▪	Golden Gate National Recreation Area Park Guide

More than 200 years ago, Gaspar de Portola became the first European to view San Francisco Bay as he and his men reached the 1200-foot-high summit of Sweeney Ridge in November 1769. Today this windswept ridge is little different—still covered with coastal scrub and grassland—from what it was when Portola first explored the area. Since then it has served as a military outpost, most recently as a Nike missile site during the 1950s, and as a part of the Golden Gate National Recreation Area. Hikes along Sweeney Ridge and close-by Milagra Ridge offer outstanding views of the Pacific Ocean, San Francisco Bay, and the mountain ranges of central San Mateo County. There are four endangered species in the Sweeney Ridge area: three butterflies—Bay Checkerspot, Mission Blue, and San Bruno Elfin—and one snake,

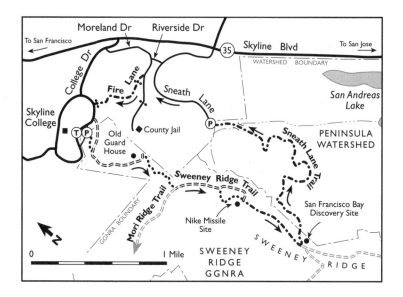

San Francisco Garter. Before your hike you may want to look these up in a field guide so that you can identify them.

Turn west on College Drive off Skyline Boulevard south of San Francisco to Skyline College. As you enter the campus, turn left and park in the first parking lot on the left. This is parking lot No. 2 and is open to visitors. From the parking lot take a right on the paved service road behind the lot and walk uphill past the maintenance barns.

The first 0.75 mile winds around the edge of a low hill on a fire road. This area is open, with occasional patches of coastal scrub.

Have the children keep a watch out for small animals and birds along here, and look up to see if any raptors (birds of prey, such as hawks and eagles) are soaring overhead.

At about 0.75 mile you come upon an old building that is in disrepair. This is a good place to rest and look out over San Francisco Bay to the east. Ask the children to guess what the building was used for (a guardhouse for the Nike missile site), and why it may have been necessary. Also ask them to imagine what the region looked like when Portola and his men first reached Sweeney Ridge and compare that with the way it looks now.

As you leave the guardhouse the trail divides and heads downhill. The trail drops 300 feet here and immediately gains it back on the other side of the ravine. You can take either branch, for they

When the feet get tired take in the view.

both lead to the creek at the bottom of this steep hillside. The trail is not well constructed here, and little has been done to build switchbacks that hold back erosion. Warn your children about sliding down the hill, and explain that switchbacks should be here to help avoid erosion and make it easier to descend the hill.

At the bottom of the hill you will cross a seasonal creek and begin an equally steep ascent up the other side. Again the trail forks, and both lead to the same spot up the hill. I prefer the left fork, for it takes you by a seepage area with small springs and vegetation that is a little thicker. If you are quiet or are out in the early morning or evening, you may see small mammals such as raccoons and foxes around the springs. Birds are always flitting around in the trees and shrubs.

The trails rejoin at the lower reaches of the ridge, and at about 1 mile the Sweeney Ridge Trail joins with the Mori Ridge Trail, which comes in from the right. Turn to your left on the wider fire road. This takes you along a slight incline through heavier coastal scrub, where there are plenty of birds and profuse blooms of wildflowers in the spring and early summer.

The fire road circles around the radar station of the old Nike missile site at just under 1.5 miles. As you approach the site a small spur trail leads off to the right, but you have easier access to the site as you round the curve just past the spur.

The fire road becomes paved at the old site, and for the next 0.5 mile or so is an easy hike on level paved road. At 2 miles you come to the San Francisco Bay Discovery Site. At this level, open site there is a stone plaque honoring Portola's expedition, and a granite monument nearby that depicts views that can be seen from this high spot on clear days. These include the Farallon Islands to the northwest, Mount Tamalpais and the Point Reyes Peninsula to the north, Mount Diablo to the northeast, and the Montara Mountains and San Pedro Point to the south.

You can return to the parking lot by the same route, or you can head downhill on the paved Sneath Lane Trail. This trail takes you about 1.25 miles to Sneath Lane, which you follow for another 0.25 mile to Riverside Drive. Take a left on Riverside and continue for a little over 0.25 mile. Just before you enter the parking area for the county jail, take a right and follow the fire lane for about 0.25 mile back to parking lot No. 2.

8   SADDLE/BOG TRAILS LOOP

Type ■	Day hike
Difficulty ■	Moderate for children
Distance ■	2.5-mile loop
Hiking time ■	2 hours
Elevation gain ■	150 feet
Hikable ■	Year-round
Map ■	San Mateo County Park

San Bruno Mountain stands as an open-space island in the midst of a densely populated urban area and offers excellent hiking opportunities with outstanding views of San Francisco, the East Bay, and the San Francisco Peninsula to the south. Support of local conservationists helped block development on the mountain and establish the area as a state and county park to protect fourteen species of rare or endangered plants and two species of endangered butterflies. The mountain, which rises to 1814 feet at the top, may be covered by fog any time of the year, and winds can be quite strong there. In the spring and early summer bright wildflowers color the slopes and plenty of birds thrive in the region. Even small mammals seem to be making a comeback here, and you can often see signs of raccoon, fox, coyote, and bobcat as you hike the trails.

All of the East Bay is visible from the slopes of San Bruno Mountain.

 Take Guadalupe Canyon Parkway west from US 101 to the exit to the park. Follow the signs, and park in the lot to the north of the parkway.

The Saddle Trail leads out to the right from the rear of the picnic area. The first portion of the trail winds through light coastal scrub as it loops around the contour of the hill. The slopes along this section are covered with profuse blooms of wildflowers in the spring and early summer. The trail levels out at about 0.5 mile, but continues around the contour of the hill. As it turns around the contour there is an excellent view of the bay and the East Bay hills. Mount Diablo is straight ahead.

At just before 0.7 mile there is a bench where you can sit and look out over the bay, the Oakland/San Francisco Bay Bridge, and downtown San Francisco.

As the trail continues around the hill it passes through a grove of eucalyptus and Monterey pine, with San Francisco still visible on the right. At the 1-mile trail marker you can take a short spur of about 100 feet out to an overlook. The view is excellent here.

The trail begins to head uphill past Vista Point. There are springs all along the hillsides here. Ask the children how you know there are springs (the lush, green growth that is very different from the surrounding plants).

At 1.25 miles a trail leads off to the left and takes you down to a day camp where there are picnic tables and water. This is a good stop if the camp is not in session, and is a return route *back* to the parking lot if your young ones are getting tired.

The trail again heads uphill from here and you soon have fine views of Twin Peaks and the Marin Headlands, with Mount Tamalpais standing high above all.

From 1.25 to 1.5 miles the trail is a roller coaster, and at 1.5 miles you come to a saddle where you begin to head downhill. At about 1.75 miles the trail follows around a chainlink fence and comes to a large eucalyptus grove. Have the children try to find some seed pods and smell some of the leaves.

The Saddle Trail dead-ends at the Old Guadalupe Trail at just before 2 miles. Take a left on the paved trail as it leads through groves of eucalyptus, willows, and brambles. There are some acacia and cypress at just past 2 miles.

The Bog Trail leads off to the right just past 2 miles. Wild strawberries grow alongside the trail. At 2.25 miles there is a bench where you can sit and look out over the bog. About 100 yards past the bench the trail splits. Either branch takes you back to the parking lot, but the trail to the right is a little wilder. Take this if your children would like to explore more, or take the left and pass over a wooden footbridge.

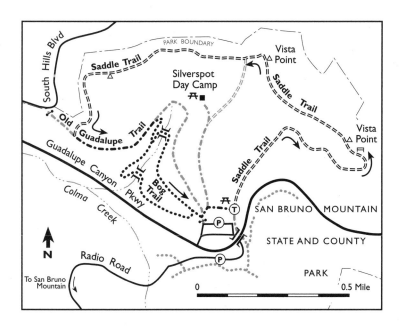

The trail passes uphill from the bog and through a grove of cypress, and there are plenty of ferns on both sides of the trail. Have the children look at the different types of fronds on the ferns.

The trail that veered to the right and went around the wild side of the bog rejoins the trail from the left at about 2.4 miles, and the Bog Trail comes back to the Old Guadalupe Trail just before you reach the parking lot.

9 QUAIL TRAIL LOOP

Type ▪	Day hike
Difficulty ▪	Moderate for children
Distance ▪	1.5-mile loop
Hiking time ▪	1 hour
Elevation gain ▪	200 feet
Hikable ▪	Year-round
Map ▪	San Mateo County Park

The 100 acres of Junipero Serra County Park are noted for the abundance of spring wildflowers, both on the open, grass-covered hillsides and in the wooded areas on the north slopes. The park is nestled into a small triangle between I-280 and the city of San Bruno. Native trees found in the park include several species of oak, California bay, buckeye, willow, and madrone. Exotics include several species of eucalyptus, Monterey cypress, and Monterey pine. Poison oak is abundant throughout the park and should be avoided.

 Take the Crystal Springs Road exit off I-280 at San Bruno and turn right on Crystal Springs Road. Continue for just over 0.5 mile to the park entrance. Turn left off Crystal Springs Road, then turn right after the tollbooth and park in the Willow Shelter parking lot. The trailhead is near the flagpole, on the east side of the parking lot.

 Live oak and poison oak cover the hills on both sides of the trails here. Wild iris are plentiful in the early spring, and native bunch grass can be seen.

Above the oak at 0.2 mile there are Monterey pines. This is about the northern extreme of their natural range.

Above them, at about 0.3 mile, there are a number of different

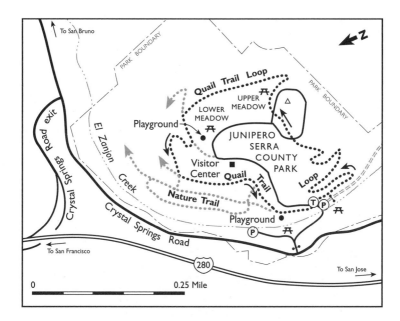

species of eucalyptus. Have the children look at the different types of leaves, seedpods, and shapes of the crowns and trunks. Even the bark is different. Have them find some different leaves. Crush them and see if they have different smells as well.

As you pass the eucalyptus, a group of pines towers above a layer of pine needles. Discuss the formation of duff and the volatility of dry pine needles, eucalyptus leaves, and chaparral. Also discuss the lack of undergrowth beneath the pine.

The trail continues uphill and passes some eucalyptus trees with multiple stems that have grown since they were either cut or frozen back. The trail twice crosses a paved road at 0.5 mile and then heads over the ridge, where you overlook San Francisco International Airport and Mount Diablo in the distance.

At just past 0.6 mile a trail leads off to a picnic area. The trail continues around the contour of the hill, and at about 0.75 mile there is a grassy meadow above the trail, with a children's playground. This is a good place to stop, because the children can play on the equipment while the adults eat, take a break, and look out over the bay. There is a grove of redwood trees downhill from the meadow.

Just before 1 mile a broad trail leads off to the left to the visitor center, and the Quail Trail Loop veers to the right. There is a large patch of poison oak alongside the trail here.

Let the kids take a break and climb on these inviting limbs.

Another fork is located just past 1 mile. The right trail leads down to a city park. Take the left on the Quail Trail Loop. This section of the trail leads through some chaparral, and a spring flows out of the hill above the trail.

At about 1.2 miles take a left at the fork where the nature trail leads off to the right. There are a number of very climbable oaks along here, but beware of the poison oak. There are also a lot of low-lying brambles alongside the trail here.

At 1.4 miles the trail comes out beside the paved road above a play area with a picnic area, climbing equipment, and volleyball courts.

As the trail returns to the parking lot you pass the trailhead for the Live Oak Nature Trail. Those with young children may prefer this 1-mile-long, self-guided loop, which is shorter and requires less climbing than the Quail Trail Loop.

10

BROOKS FALLS OVERLOOK TRAIL/OLD TROUT FARM TRAILS LOOP

Type ■	Day hike
Difficulty ■	Moderate for children
Distance ■	1.5-mile loop
Hiking time ■	1 hour
Elevation gain ■	150 feet
Hikable ■	Year-round
Map ■	San Mateo County Park

The 1150-acre San Pedro Valley County Park has two freshwater creeks that flow year-round through lush valleys. These are the south and middle forks of San Pedro Creek, and both are significant because they provide some of the rare spawning areas for migratory steelhead in San Mateo County. The spawning season is generally between December and February. During this time, and until the end of the rainy season, the 175-foot-high, three-tiered

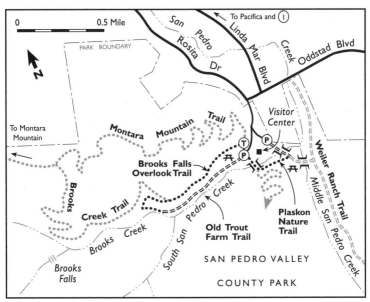

Brooks Falls is a special attraction along the south fork of the creek. Many sensitive plants live in the streamside habitat provided in the park, with several different trilliums, many fern species, creek dogwood, and arroyo willow all found along the creek banks. The slopes and meadows offer a colorful array of wildflowers in the spring. An abundance of birds and small mammals live in the park. The short (0.03-mile) Plaskon Nature Trail is a good introduction to the plant life of the park and should be taken before beginning the longer Brooks Falls Overlook Trail/Old Trout Farm Trail Loop.

Take Linda Mar Boulevard off CA 1 in Pacifica, and continue until it dead-ends at Oddstad Boulevard. Take a right turn on Oddstad, and the entrance to the park is about 50 yards on the left. Park in the lot to the right of the visitor center. The Plaskon Nature Trail is behind the visitor center, and the Brooks Falls Overlook Trail begins behind the rest rooms at the rear of the parking lot.

The falls are just beyond the curve.

Before starting your hike, you may wish to take a walk to the rear of the visitor center where the short, self-guided Plaskon Nature Trail introduces you to the various plants found in the park.

After taking the nature trail you can head uphill on the Brooks Falls Overlook Trail. For the first 0.25 mile the trail leads along the contour of the hill through a mixed forest with several exotics such as eucalyptus and Monterey pine. There is heavy undergrowth here, including thick stands of poison oak.

After about 0.25 mile the trail begins a steeper climb up the hillside through a thick stand of eucalyptus. Although there are some old, large trees in this grove, there are also many very young ones. Talk to the children about how the eucalyptus reproduce very rapidly when the conditions are right, and obviously there were several years in the past decade where those conditions were excellent, for these stands of young trees are very defined.

At about 0.5 mile there is a bench on the uphill side of the trail that overlooks the deep canyon of Brooks Creek and to the right offers an excellent view of the three-tiered Brooks Falls (or it does when the falls are active). Immediately past the bench you will see a trail that leads off to the right. Do not take that trail, but head downhill to the left.

The trail leads downhill, where it crosses a feeder creek and levels out as it follows the contour of the hill on the opposite side of the creek. The trail leads into an area that was obviously once a homestead. There are steps, concrete retaining walls, and some paths that are left of what was a large home. Just below the homesite, after you have descended down some stone steps, you will find the remains of a garden and some old garden ponds.

At about 0.75 mile the trail winds around to follow Brooks Creek until it joins South San Pedro Creek. Although there are several spots along the creek where children can explore, including one where a fallen tree spans the creek, caution them that this is a spawning creek for migratory steelhead, and that their spawning grounds should not be disturbed. Brooks Creek joins South San Pedro Creek at about 1 mile, and the trail becomes Old Trout Farm Trail as you turn left. This section of the trail is a wide road that once led to a trout farm in the area; it follows along the creek. Again, there are several access points, but caution the children to only look and not disturb the steelhead.

The trail returns to the parking lot and picnic area at 1.5 miles.

11

JAMES V. FITZGERALD MARINE RESERVE TRAIL LOOP

Type ▪	Day hike
Difficulty ▪	Moderate for children
Distance ▪	1-mile loop
Hiking time ▪	1 hour
Elevation gain ▪	50 feet
Hikable ▪	Year-round
Map ▪	San Mateo County Park

The reefs and marine life have been studied in James V. Fitzgerald Marine Reserve for more than seventy years, and twenty-five species of invertebrates and plants that were new to science have been discovered here. In addition, there are several endemic species (ones that live nowhere else) found here. The reserve was set aside in 1969 to protect the fragile and complex marine communities so that we—and future generations—can enjoy them. The reefs offer excellent tide pools for exploration, especially during low tides. All marine life is protected within the reserve except for some game fish, so do not collect specimens.

Hikes along shoreline cliffs offer panoramic views.

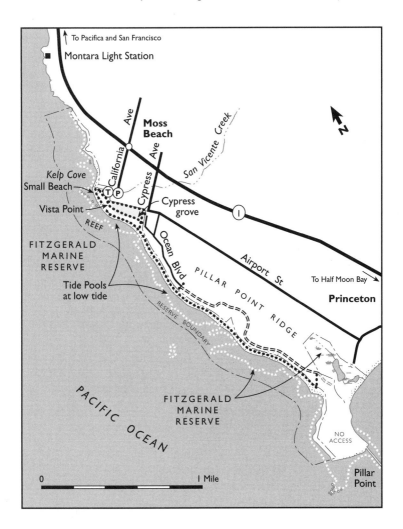

Follow the signs in Moss Beach (CA 1 to California Avenue) to the reserve parking lot. From the parking lot head down the paved trail toward the beach, but take the trail to the left over the wooden footbridge. After about 100 feet the trail takes you to a lookout point, where a wooden fence keeps hikers from getting too close to the edge of the sandstone cliffs.

From the vista point follow the trail south along the fence and through a cypress grove. At 0.5 mile the trail begins to descend to the beach. If the tide is too high to follow the bottom of the cliffs along the reefs, you must retrace your route after a stop on the beach at the south end of the reserve.

If the tide is low you can take a walk along the bottom of the cliffs, explore the many tide pools, and climb over the rocks. The best tide pools are obviously at very low tide, but there are some worth exploring any time the reefs are exposed at all. On the day I was there (it was not a particularly low tide) a great blue heron stood in one of the pools for the entire time, hunting for fish and small marine invertebrates.

Have the children search around the tide pools to see if they can find any starfish, sea anemones, hermit crabs, or other small marine animals that live in this tidal zone. When they spot a sea anemone have them gently place their fingers in the center of the anemone to see how it closes up to capture prey. Starfish may be gently lifted from the water so that the children can feel their rough surfaces and see the suction cups on the bottoms of their arms.

You return to a more open beach at about 0.75 mile. You can take a break and play there, or you can hike past it to Kelp Cove where you may see some seals and various water birds.

12 PULGAS RIDGE OPEN SPACE PRESERVE TRAIL LOOP

Type	▪ Day hike
Difficulty	▪ Moderate for children
Distance	▪ 2-mile loop
Hiking time	▪ 2 hours
Elevation gain	▪ 400 feet
Hikable	▪ Year-round
Map	▪ Midpeninsula Regional Open Space District

Cordilleras Creek originates in the canyons of this open space preserve, and a broad, high meadow sits between two wooded canyons. During the spring this is one of the premier wildflower sites on the peninsula. The 293 acres in the preserve lie just north of Edgewood County Park, and feature many of the same animal and bird habitats and plant communities.

Some prefer jogging; others prefer a casual stroll.

Take the Edgewood Road exit off I-280 and head east for 1 mile. Turn left on Crestview Road and take another left immediately on Edmonds Road. Park at a roadside turnout after the first curve on Edmonds.

To begin the hike, from the turnout take a right through the gate and walk just over 0.5 mile on a paved easement road through a valley owned by the San Francisco Water District. As you reach the gate to the preserve, the road turns left and then heads uphill to the high meadow where a tuberculosis hospital once stood.

The meadow is now encircled by an oak forest and is filled with brilliant wildflowers in the spring. It is a good spot to have a picnic on warm spring or fall days.

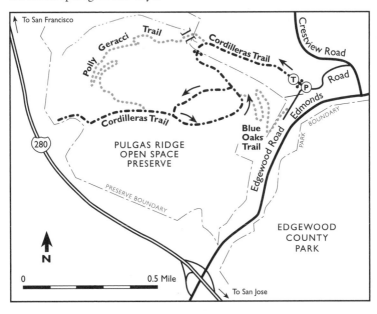

From the meadow the paved road continues to the top of the preserve at just over 1 mile, where there are views of canyons on both sides of the ridges. During the spring wildflower bloom; this is an impressive site.

During the long blooming season here have the children keep track of the many different species of flowers they find along the trail. Help them spot small, low-lying flowers that they might miss without bending low and searching diligently.

Remember, you don't have to know the names of the flowers to enjoy their beauty. In fact, children love to give their own names to flowers and later compare them with those given in field guides.

Walk to the end of the paved road near the water tank and return, following the road around the other side of the meadow to the parking area.

13 EDGEWOOD/RIDGEVIEW/ SYLVAN TRAILS LOOP

Type ■	Day hike
Difficulty ■	Difficult for children
Distance ■	5-mile loop
Hiking time ■	3 hours
Elevation gain ■	600 feet
Hikable ■	Year-round
Map ■	San Mateo County Park

The open grasslands in Edgewood County Park sit on serpentine hills and are famous for their spring wildflower displays. In addition, the 407 park acres feature oak woodlands and chaparral plant communities that are home to many small mammals and dozens of species of birds. Seven rare or endangered plant species have been identified in the park. These include the San Francisco thornmint, which was thought to be extinct for a number of years. The bay checkerspot butterfly, which once was plentiful around the entire Bay Area, is now found only in this park and two others: Jasper Ridge and San Bruno Mountain.

Take the Edgewood Road exit off I-280 and head east for 1 mile to the park entrance. Turn right at the Edgewood Park and Day

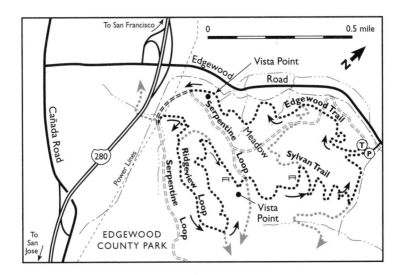

Camp sign and cross the bridge to the parking lot. The trailhead is on the west side of the lot.

Edgewood Trail begins a steep uphill climb out of the parking lot and leads through a mixed forest with buckeye, oak, and madrone. A thick undergrowth of toyon and poison oak covers the ground on both sides of the trail.

A service road crosses the trail just past 0.25 mile. Edgewood levels out somewhat along this section, and the uphill slope is a grass-covered meadow filled with brilliant wildflowers during the spring.

The trail continues to climb slowly through a shaded oak/madrone forest, and at about 0.5 mile the Sylvan Trail leads off to the left. If you feel that the young ones in your party won't be able to make the full 5 miles of this hike, this makes a good turnaround. A left on Sylvan back to the parking lot makes about a 1.75-mile loop along wood-shaded trails.

For those who wish to make the entire loop, continue straight. The trail hugs the steep contours of the canyons that drain the northwest side of the park, and the steep canyons are blanketed with a thick cover of bay trees.

At about 1 mile the trail leaves the shade of the forests and enters an area of open grassland on the uphill side and a stand of chaparral on the downhill side. Here a spur trail leads off to the right for about 100 feet, and there is a small knoll with large rocks, which makes a good picnic and rest stop. The views from here are good, and the wildflowers are spectacular in the spring.

The children may wish to explore around the rocks for lizards, but let them know that there are rattlesnakes in the park. They should not stick their hands into any crevices where they do not have a good view, and they should be careful before sitting on any rocks.

After the rest stop, the trail heads downhill, passes another service road that crosses the grassland, goes under a power line, and becomes part of the Serpentine Loop. At just under 2 miles Edgewood Trail ends. The single track Serpentine Loop continues straight ahead at this junction and crosses a creek area with good stands of willow. To your left the Ridgeview Loop heads uphill into a wooded area.

Colorful flowers add to the beauty of the hillside.

You may wish to continue to the creek area, where there are large numbers of birds, especially during the nesting season, and backtrack to Ridgeview before heading uphill. Children like to explore along the edge of this marshy area.

Ridgeview Loop leads up a small canyon through grassland, and then turns uphill toward an oak forest. After about 200 yards there is a fork, with a trail leading off to the left. If your party is getting tired, you can take this trail to cut about 1 mile off the loop. It leads around the north slope of the ridge, while the other leads around the south.

Take the right fork to complete the loop. The trail leads through a forest of large trees and out into an open hillside by 2.5 miles. Uphill is a stand of chaparral, and to the right is a fantastic view of open grass meadows dotted with multiple hues of wildflowers in the spring.

At about 2.75 miles the trail comes to a junction. Straight ahead takes you to the Serpentine Loop. Take the left to head along the top of the ridge through a heavy growth of chaparral. Have the children discuss why the shrubs of the chaparral are so much smaller than the oak and bay of the rest of the park.

After several hundred yards of chaparral, the trail again enters an oak forest and begins to descend.

At about 3 miles Ridgeview Loop dead-ends. Take a right on Sylvan Trail and continue downhill. In this stretch you can see the meadow that the Serpentine Loop traverses; there is a bench where you can stop and enjoy the view at about 3.25 miles.

There is a trail junction at about 3.5 miles where the Sylvan Trail crosses the Serpentine Loop. Continue straight ahead on the Sylvan Trail as you cross the open grassland and head for another canopy of oak and buckeye.

Just before 4 miles the trail splits. The trail to the left leads back to the Edgewood Trail, and the one to the right is the Sylvan Trail that leads back to the parking lot. Take the right fork, which goes downhill. The next mile leads you through a thick forest that offers shade from the hot afternoon sun, which makes the other trails somewhat uncomfortable on warm days.

14 ZWIERLEIN/RICHARD'S ROAD/ DEAN TRAILS LOOP

Type ▪	Day hike
Difficulty ▪	Moderate for children
Distance ▪	2-mile loop
Hiking time ▪	2 hours
Elevation gain ▪	250 feet
Hikable ▪	Year-round
Map ▪	San Mateo County Park

This trail loop in Huddart County Park gives an in-depth look at the deep canyons where tall redwoods tower over an almost enchanted forest of ferns and low-lying plants. Between 1853 and 1860 five sawmills operated near the present-day boundaries of Huddart County Park, as the huge, old-growth redwoods of

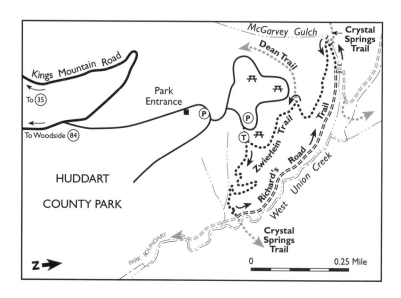

the area were harvested to help meet the demand for lumber in booming San Francisco. It has been more than 100 years since the forests were logged, and the rejuvenated forest covers much of the evidence of that activity. A new forest of redwoods has grown up around the large stumps that are all that was left of the original virgin forests. A section of the trail on this hike, Richard's Road Trail, follows along the old road, where the lumber was transported to Redwood City to waiting barges, which carried the lumber to San Francisco.

Take the Woodside exit off I-280 and head west on Woodside Road for about 2 miles. Turn right on Kings Mountain Road and go about 1.5 miles to the park entrance. Continue past the first parking lot on the left to the Zwierlein Picnic Area. The trailhead is just to the south of the rest rooms.

Take the Zwierlein Trail to the right downhill through chaparral and into a small redwood grove. After about 0.1 mile the trail begins a series of sharp switchbacks down through an oak/madrone/bay forest. On the left side of the trail notice some redwood rings where young trees have sprouted from the roots of an old stump.

Many of the bay trees are multitrunked. Ask the children how they may have gotten that way. (Most of the young plants were eaten or broken off and new trunks were formed.)

Many different types of large and small ferns also grow along the trail. Have the children see how many they can spot.

The Zwierlein Trail continues downhill alongside a steadily deepening canyon until it dead-ends into the Richard's Road Trail at about 0.5 mile. At this point take a left on Richard's Road Trail and head along the banks of West Union Creek. The trail is now a wide, well-maintained dirt road.

For the next 0.5 mile the trail leads by several rock outcroppings where you can take rest stops and look down over the creek, or scramble down the creek bank to explore the water's edge.

The canyon rises sharply to the left of the trail as you make a slow climb toward the confluence of West Union Creek and McGarvey Gulch Creek, which occurs in about 0.75 mile.

Watch for that shaft of sunlight that highlights the green undergrowth.

Several hundred yards past the confluence of the two creeks, Richard's Road Trail takes a sharp right turn across a large rock bridge to head up the hill on the opposite side of McGarvey Gulch Creek. Continue straight ahead here, as the trail becomes a narrow footpath heading upstream. This is a good rest stop where the children have easy access to the creek.

After another 50 yards the Crystal Springs Trail crosses the creek to the right. Stay to the left on what is now Dean Trail. This trail immediately begins to head uphill on switchbacks. You soon move away from the creek and into a mixed forest with fir, oak, madrone, and bay.

At 1.75 miles the Zwierlein Trail leads off to the left. Take it and continue around the contour of the hill for 0.25 mile until you return to the trailhead.

15
EL CORTE DE MADERA CREEK TRAIL

Type ▪	Day hike
Difficulty ▪	Moderate for children
Distance ▪	2 or 3 miles, round trip
Hiking time ▪	2 hours
Elevation gain ▪	300 feet
Hikable ▪	Year-round
Map ▪	Midpeninsula Regional Open Space District

El Corte de Madera Creek rises from springs near Skyline Boulevard and flows between high ridges along the west side of El Corte de Madera Open Space Preserve. This preserve, with elevations ranging from the 2400-foot summit of Sierra Morena to the 700-foot elevation at the bottom of the canyon where the creek leaves the preserve on the west side, is a place of deep canyons and exposed ridges. The high ridges and deep canyons offer contrasting, but equally breathtaking, views. The redwood forests were first logged in the 1860s and logging continued until the late 1980s when the Open Space District acquired the 2700 acres.

Heading south on Skyline Boulevard continue past Skeggs Point about 0.25 mile to Gate CM02 on the right side of the road. Park

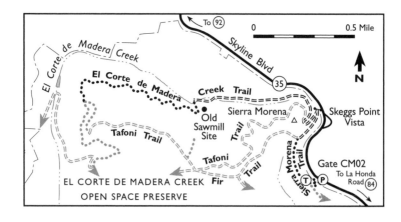

Kids explore the creek banks during break time.

at the trailhead of the Sierra Morena Trail. The trailhead is about 3 miles from CA 84 heading north. From the trailhead take the Sierra Morena Trail north for about 0.25 miles past the junction with the Fir Trail to the beginning of the El Corte de Madera Creek Trail.

Take a left on the old logging road and head downhill. You pass through an open area where signs of logging still abound, but by 0.75 mile you reach a forest of fir and redwood that stands high above the creek.

At about 1.0 mile a small creek merges with El Corte de Madera Creek from the left. This was the site of one of the earliest sawmills in the canyon, which operated in the late 1800s. This is the stopping point if you want a 2-mile round trip, and is a perfect place for a picnic. You can discuss with your children the logging activities here in the late 1800s, and talk about how our attitudes about logging have changed in the past century or so. The children can also explore the creek banks as you rest.

You can return by the same route for a 2-mile hike, but if the children are up for a longer hike you can continue on the trail as it crosses the creek and heads into a cool, moist canyon where ferns along the creek grow taller, and brilliant wildflowers dot the banks from May through August.

If you choose this longer hike you will continue along El Corte de Madera Creek Trail for another 0.75 mile to its junction with the Tafoni Trail. Take a left on the Tafoni Trail and continue for another 0.5 mile to the junction with Fir Trail. Veer right onto Fir Trail and head for the junction with Sierra Morena Trail, where you take a right back to the trailhead. This hike will be a little less than 3 miles.

16 BEAR GULCH/REDWOOD/ MADRONE TRAILS LOOP

Type ■	Day hike
Difficulty ■	Difficult for children
Distance ■	3-mile loop
Hiking time ■	2 hours
Elevation gain ■	600 feet
Hikable ■	Year-round
Map ■	San Mateo County Park

This hike follows the northern boundary of Wunderlich County Park through chaparral and mixed conifer forest to Redwood Flat. There the trail leads to Salamander Flat before heading back downhill through a dense grove of redwoods. Alambique Creek was the primary source of water for the area's early settlers, and they eventually built a reservoir at Salamander Flat. Water was then piped downhill to the residents. Today the reservoir is a picnic site and salamander breeding ground rather than a water supply, and hikers are often surprised to come upon the sheltered pond as they hike along the ridge.

Take the Woodside Road (CA 84) exit off I-280 and head southwest on Woodside Road for 2 miles. The small sign that marks the entrance to the park is on the right-hand side of the road. The trailhead for this hike is located uphill from the parking lot behind the large old barn.

The Bear Gulch Trail begins a steep ascent with switchbacks up through a mixed oak and madrone forest. Some chaparral can be seen on the downhill side of the trail. This is a favorite equestrian trail, and it can be a bit narrow when you meet a large horse on one

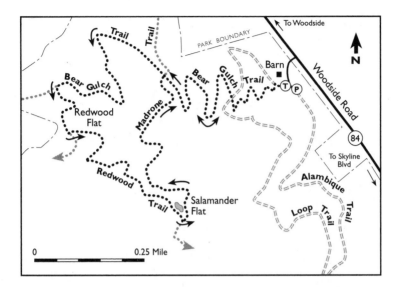

of the switchbacks. Remind your children about getting out of the way and not making any quick movements that might spook the horses.

At about 0.5 mile the Bear Gulch Trail crosses the Madrone Trail. Horses aren't allowed on Bear Gulch Trail past Madrone Trail during the winter months, and that makes the trail more enjoyable for hikers. Between 0.5 and 1 mile the trail winds upward at a steady pace, and through a good grove of second-growth redwood. At about 0.75 mile there are remains of several very large redwood stumps left from some long-ago forest fire. Children often like to play in these and pretend they are forts or other imaginary places.

Near 1 mile a spur leads off to the right of the main trail, but keep to the left as the trail approaches a road outside the park boundaries.

Just past 1 mile at Redwood Flat, Redwood Trail leads off to the left. Take this trail as it winds around the contour of the canyons. For the next 0.5 mile the trail is fairly level but winding. Steep canyons are on the left side of the trail as it passes through large redwoods.

At Salamander Flat at 1.5 miles there is a pleasant surprise for all. A good-sized reservoir that once served residents below now sits, full, on the left side of the trail just before the junction with the Madrone Trail. It is not a swimming hole, for the sides drop off quickly to deep water, but it is an excellent picnic site where the

Reminders of fires long extinguished

children can search for the many salamanders that can be found there at various times of the year. This was a favorite breeding spot for them even before the reservoir was built.

As you leave the reservoir, head downhill on the Madrone Trail. It winds steadily down through large stands of redwoods that furnish cool shade and moisture for the many ferns and other shade-loving plants. Large redwoods often capture their own water from the summer fogs that frequently cover the hills and mountains around the San Francisco Bay. This captured water is often equal to an additional 8 to 10 inches of rain each year.

Just before 2.75 miles you reach the intersection of the Madrone Trail with the Bear Gulch Trail. Take a right onto the Bear Gulch Trail to return to the barn.

17 COOLEY LANDING TRAIL LOOP

Type ▪ Day hike
Difficulty ▪ Easy for children
Distance ▪ 2.5-miles, round trip
Hiking time ▪ 1 hour
Elevation gain ▪ None
Hikable ▪ Year-round
Maps ▪ USGS topographics—Palo Alto and Mountain View

There are more than 2 miles of broad marshes that extend from Menlo Park to Palo Alto along the shores of San Francisco Bay. A number of paths, boardwalks, and viewing platforms allow hikers and walkers to enjoy the views and to observe close-up the plant and animal life that abounds in tidal marshes and mudflats. Cooley Landing in east Palo Alto is one of the few restored areas of this marshland. There, a boardwalk and paths lead you through and around tidal marshes, open water, and a slough where you have an excellent opportunity to view a wide variety of bird life.

Take the University Avenue exit north off US 101 in Palo Alto. After less than 0.5 mile, turn right on Bay Road, and head east until the road dead-ends at the parking area at Cooley Landing.

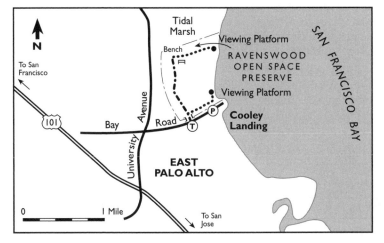

When near marshes, keep an eye out for wading birds

Start this trail along the dikes of the salt pond on the north side of the slough at the plaza at Cooley Landing. Begin by heading west on Bay Road away from the bay for about 200 yards. Cross the bridge over the slough to your right and follow the levee straight ahead. The levee bends as it follows around the slough, and to your right is one of many salt ponds built in the south San Francisco Bay during the late 1800s and early 1900s.

The paved trail ends at about 0.75 mile, where a bench offers a rest spot and a good place to look out over the marsh. The children can explore the edge of the levee and look for small animals and birds that live nearby. One bird that lives here is seldom seen, but is an exciting find if it is spotted by you or the children. This is the clapper rail, a well-camouflaged—and endangered—water bird that survives in the various preserves and refuges around San Francisco Bay.

After taking a break, continue another 0.25 mile to a viewing platform where you can look out over the bay to watch the water-fowl and shorebirds that feed here. From the platform you can see another platform just to the south, but the old trail to it has been closed. To reach it you must backtrack to the trailhead and head out on another short trail. After seeing other busily feeding birds it is only a short walk back to the parking lot from the platform.

18

WINDY HILL SUMMIT TRAIL LOOP

Type ▪	Day hike
Difficulty ▪	Easy for children
Distance ▪	0.75-mile loop
Hiking time ▪	1 hour
Elevation gain ▪	130 feet
Hikable ▪	Year-round
Map ▪	Midpeninsula Regional Open Space District

The Windy Hill Open Space Preserve includes two bald knobs that stand high above Portola Valley. Hikers who climb the short trail to the tops of the bald knobs have a 360-degree view of the Pacific, San Francisco Bay, distant mountains, and many cities. In the summer, wind and fog are common occurrences here and the views are blocked by the fog banks at times, but a visit to this preserve is always bracing and invigorating. Some 14 miles of trails traverse the 1181-acre preserve, crossing grass-covered meadows, climbing steep slopes to ridgelines, and following stream canyons. The short trail to the tops of the bald knobs is one of the most popular; it gives a good overview of the 8.5-mile Windy Hill Trail Loop, one of the longest loop trails on the peninsula.

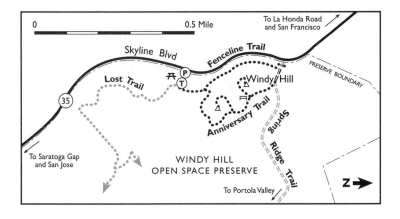

The main entrance to the preserve is located on the east side of Skyline Boulevard, 2 miles south of La Honda Road. The trailhead is on the north side of the picnic area.

There are a number of longer hikes in this preserve, but this short loop takes you to a top-of-the-world view of the San Francisco Bay area. Take the trail to the left from the Skyline Boulevard picnic area toward the knobs of Windy Hill. This is a well-marked trail, and the knobs are in view the whole time.

The knobs are open, grass-covered landmarks, and on the less than 0.5-mile trail to the top, many San Francisco region peaks come into view. At the top you can see Black Mountain, Mount Hamilton, Mount Diablo, and Mount Tamalpais.

In addition, you can see the ocean to the west and San Francisco Bay, with its many surrounding cities, to the east.

Have the children try to pick out some of the peaks and cities, and if you live within view, try to find your neighborhood.

Return to the parking lot by the same trail, or take the one down the opposite side of the knobs for a loop.

Boulders are for climbing, but make sure you know what's on the other side.

19 HORSESHOE LAKE TRAIL LOOP

Type ▪	Day hike
Difficulty ▪	Easy for children
Distance ▪	1.5-mile loop
Hiking time ▪	1 hour
Elevation gain ▪	100 feet
Hikable ▪	Year-round
Map ▪	Midpeninsula Regional Open Space District

Another of the multitude of open space preserves and parks found along Skyline Boulevard, Skyline Ridge Open Space Preserve has 1200 acres that include a Christmas tree farm, two small reservoirs, and a 2493-foot knoll that is unnamed. Rolling grasslands cover the upper regions of the preserve, and the steep slopes of the lower regions are covered by mixed conifer forests. For hundreds of years Native Americans lived in the region and gathered acorns from the oak forests. Some of the bedrock grinding stones they used to grind acorns can still be seen in the preserve. Settlers

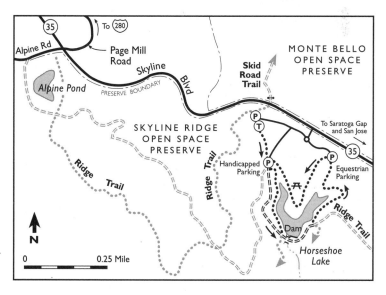

Even the shores of old reservoirs make for interesting hikes.

came to the area as early as 1850 and built ranch houses along the ridge.

Park at the preserve entrance located on Skyline Boulevard, less than 1 mile southeast of Alpine Road. Take the old farm road that heads downhill from the parking area.

The road descends into a small valley that lies to the east of the steep slopes that drop down from the preserve's summit. The road goes through open grassland that has an occasional oak, and you can soon see the U-shaped Horseshoe Lake that wraps around a knoll with trees jutting from its top.

At 0.5 mile the road ends and trails fork to the right and left. Take the right and continue for 200 yards to the south end of the lake. Cross the earthen dam and take the path around the marsh at the rim of the lake. The children can explore along the edges of this marsh for signs of wildlife and look for small birds that live there. During nesting season in particular you should see and hear a number of birds, including redwing blackbirds. Frogs abound here also.

In early morning or evening you may see deer, raccoon, fox, and maybe even a bobcat as they come to drink at the lake. These animals inhabit the surrounding woods and are rarely seen, except at the lake and in the open meadows.

At 0.75 mile the trail leads to the top of the knoll, where picnic tables sit. Take a pleasant break here as the children explore around the lake.

After you have rested, continue on around the knoll to head back north to complete the loop.

2O BIG TREE TRAIL

Type ▪	Day hike
Difficulty ▪	Moderate for children
Distance ▪	1.5-mile loop
Hiking time ▪	1 hour
Elevation gain ▪	250 feet
Hikable ▪	Year-round
Map ▪	San Mateo County Park

Sam McDonald County Park is part of the much larger park complex that includes Pescadero Creek County Park, Memorial County Park, Heritage Grove Redwood Preserve, and Portola State Park. Together these include nearly 10,000 acres of redwood and mixed conifer forests, steep canyons carved by roaring streams, and miles of trails. The streams are lush with stands of ferns, and the ridges and high meadows are covered with rolling grasslands and chaparral and have abundant wildflowers during the spring. Wildlife is plentiful throughout the parks, but more so in the high meadows and chaparral country. Some of the largest coast redwoods in the San Francisco Bay region can be found in the groves of these parks.

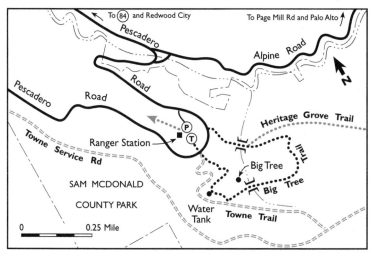

Even the limbs on this giant are huge.

Park in the parking area at the ranger station of Sam McDonald County Park off Pescadero Road, about 0.5 mile west of the junction of Pescadero and Alpine Roads.

From the parking lot take the trail that crosses Pescadero Road to the Big Tree Trail. Be careful crossing the road because there are curves on both sides of the crosswalk.

The trail begins on the fire road that heads uphill, and during the first 0.25 mile crosses over the road several times. Sometimes it follows the road, at other times it becomes a narrow trail alongside it.

Along this section you will see a number of good-sized redwoods and old stumps of even larger ones that were cut down during the late 1800s. Have the children explore some of the old stumps and see if they can calculate how old the trees may have been when they were cut. Children also may "guestimate" the number of rings they can count within, say, 5 inches, and then extrapolate that out to the number that might be in the whole stump.

The trail climbs steadily here, and at about 0.5 mile the road passes by a large water tank on the left; the trail leads off the road to the left into large redwoods just past the tank. This is the real beginning of the Big Tree Trail loop, where you will find the largest of the large. The trail follows the contour of the hills along this section and stays relatively level.

At just past 0.75 mile you round a curve in the trail and come upon what is probably the largest redwood tree found in this grove—maybe even one of the largest found in San Mateo County.

You are uphill from it as it rises from the creek bed below, and you can see that one of its limbs alone, which grows upward like a trunk, is as large as many of the second-growth redwood in the park. Find the bench beside the trail so that you can sit, look, and wonder about the life span of this magnificent tree.

Just past the bench the trail curves to the left, begins to descend, and crosses a footbridge over the creek. It climbs again on the other side and you have another view of the huge redwood. From this side you can see where it rises from the ground, which makes it seem even larger.

By 1 mile the trail heads downhill as it leads through a more open understory. It winds around the contour of the hill and returns to Pescadero Road at just under 1.5 miles. Cross the road and return to the parking area.

21 MOUNT ELLEN NATURE TRAIL

Type ▪	Day hike
Difficulty ▪	Moderate for children
Distance ▪	1 mile
Hiking time ▪	1 hour
Elevation gain ▪	300 feet
Hikable ▪	Year-round
Map ▪	San Mateo County Park

Memorial County Park is the oldest unit in the San Mateo County Park system. It was acquired in 1924 as a memorial to the men of San Mateo County who lost their lives in World War I. It is exhibiting degradation because of its long history and overuse, but its trails still offer excellent introductions to the varied and complex natural history of the Santa Cruz Mountains.

Redwood sorrel makes for a green carpet in the undergrowth of redwoods.

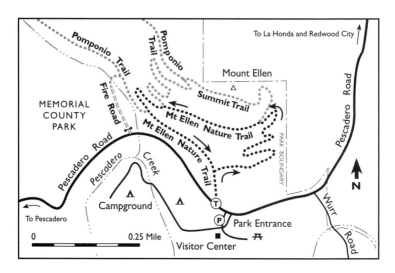

Park in the lot at the park entrance and ranger station off Pescadero Road, about 3.5 miles west of the junction of Pescadero and Alpine Roads. Pick up a self-guiding brochure to the Mount Ellen Nature Trail at the visitor center just inside the park before crossing Pescadero Road to the beginning of the Mount Ellen Nature Trail.

This self-guided nature trail begins with a gentle climb through a batch of redwood forest understory, with huckleberry bushes, some brambles, and ferns. After about 0.1 mile the route begins a series of switchbacks uphill through second-growth redwoods, some of which form almost perfect circles around old stumps. Have the children discuss how these circles of trees formed (sprouted from the roots of old trees that were cut or died). Mention that these can be found throughout redwood forests, and that this is only one of several ways that redwoods regenerate. The others include sprouting from seeds and growing directly from the stumps.

One of the best examples of these redwood circles is found at just before 0.25 mile. The children can climb uphill from the trail to stand in the midst of the circle and look skyward to get a good feel for the height of the trees.

Just past 0.25 mile the trail turns sharply to the left and follows a fairly straight and level path along the side of the hill through a mixed forest of redwood, fir, madrone, and oak. Just before 0.5 mile the trail to the top of Mount Ellen takes off to the right. This loop adds a little over 0.5 mile and about 300 feet to the hike. If your children would like to climb to the peak, take this trail; otherwise, continue straight ahead on the nature trail loop.

Around 0.75 mile several seasonal creeks cross the trail, and some large trees that have been uprooted by the roaring waters during winter storms lie beside the trail. Ask the children how these trees were uprooted, and tell them about the power of rushing water.

The trail continues around the hill and takes a sharp turn back to the trailhead just past 0.75 mile. The return trail follows above a canyon where large California bay and redwood trees are located.

Return to the parking area across the road after reaching the trailhead.

22 BUTANO CREEK TRAIL LOOP

Type ▪	Day hike
Difficulty ▪	Moderate to difficult for children
Distance ▪	2.5-mile loop
Hiking time ▪	3 hours
Elevation gain ▪	400 feet
Hikable ▪	Year-round
Map ▪	Butano State Park

The 2186 acres of redwoods in Butano State Park were destined to be logged in the 1950s when conservationists joined together in a successful fight to preserve this outstanding grove. The steep canyons in the park are covered with majestic redwoods that provide shade for the many ferns and other shade-loving plants commonly found in redwood forests. In the winter this area is often the scene of heavy rains, and the creeks fill with roiling water carrying debris, limbs, and small logs. Some winters even large logs cascade down the canyons, wiping out small trees and bridges as the swift-moving streams rise above normal levels. The evidence of this power can be seen along the Butano Creek Trail.

From CA 1 take Pescadero Road 2.5 miles to Cloverdale Road. Turn south on Cloverdale Road and continue for 4.5 miles to the park entrance. Once in the park continue on the main paved road for just under 1 mile to a turnout on the left side of the road at the Butano Creek trailhead.

Count the different types of ferns as you hike along forest creek banks.

To begin the hike take a left from the parking area as the trail leads up Butano Creek. Have the children talk about some of the ways you can tell which direction a stream or creek is flowing. They may wish to drop a leaf in the water to make sure you are heading upstream.

For the first 0.25 mile you walk with the creek on your left, and then you cross over to the other side on a wooden footbridge. This bridge is occasionally washed out by floodwaters. Have the children try to imagine how the water must appear during such times, and discuss what damage could be done along the banks of the creeks and on the slopes above. The trail continues along the creek until 0.75 mile and passes by numerous large redwoods and many signs of flood damage, including large trees uprooted on the hillsides and logs stuck in curves of the creek as they were pushed downstream during the floods.

At about 0.75 mile the trail crosses the creek in several places that are impassable during high water, making this portion of the trail inaccessible after heavy winter rains. Some bridges in this section are portable ones that are taken down after the rains begin and are replaced after the water level lowers in the spring or early summer.

Just before 1 mile the trail leads away from the creek and quickly climbs the steep slope above the creek. Have the children walk cautiously along some stretches here; a slip off the side of the trail can lead to a tumble down the slope for several hundred feet.

Just past 1 mile the trail descends to the creek again and crosses it on a large bridge that was once used by loggers. The trail continues on a logging road and makes a steady climb to the top of the ridge far above the creek below. The forests here are more mixed than the redwood and bay forests by the creek, and they have a more open understory.

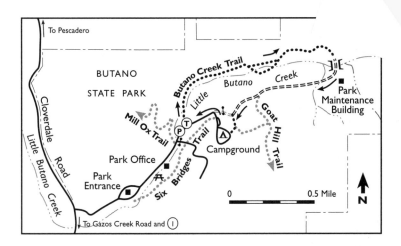

At about 1.25 miles the road passes by a building used by the park maintenance staff, then levels out and begins a slow descent. Just past 1.5 miles you pass a trail that leads off to the left to the campground. Several hundred yards later you enter a portion of the campground before joining the paved road that leads back to the parking area.

Continue downhill on the paved road as it winds below the campground to the trailhead on Butano Creek at about 2.5 miles.

23 PESCADERO MARSH TRAIL LOOP

Type ▪	Day hike
Difficulty ▪	Easy for children
Distance ▪	1.75-mile loop
Hiking time ▪	1 hour
Elevation gain ▪	Minimal
Hikable ▪	Year-round
Map ▪	Butano State Park

Pescadero Marsh Natural Preserve contains more than 500 acres of coastal wetlands, the largest wetland area between San Francisco Bay and Elkhorn Slough near Watsonville. More than 100 species

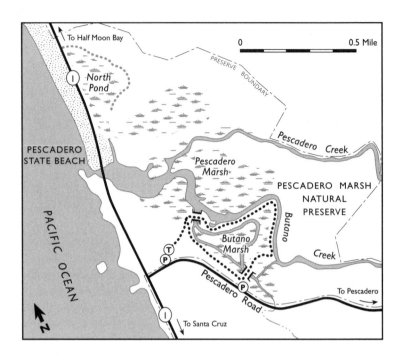

of animals and 380 species of plants are found in the marsh area, and many migrating birds use the marsh as a layover point as they fly along the Pacific Flyway each fall and spring. The marsh was formed about 6500 years ago at the end of the last Ice Age, and the first humans to inhabit the area around the marsh were the Ohlone Indians. They were part of a group of Native Americans who lived between what is now Monterey and San Francisco as long 10,000 years ago. They used the marsh and surrounding country as a source of food, such as wild herbs, clams, fish, shellfish, elk, deer, and sea mammals. When the first Spanish explorers came to the area in 1774, thousands of trout and salmon swam in the streams and marsh. Wolves and grizzly bears stalked the forests on the surrounding hills. By the 1850s a small town was established southeast of the marsh, and activity has continued in the region ever since.

The marsh lies at the northeast corner of CA 1 and Pescadero Road, 17 miles south of Half Moon Bay. For this hike, park in the pullout along the north side of Pescadero Road about 200 yards off CA 1. The trail leads out from the rear of the pullout.

The first 0.25 mile of the trail leads through a covering of coastal

Follow the levees through marsh areas where wildlife abounds.

scrub where many small birds flit about. At 0.25 mile the trail comes to an end at a larger, better maintained path. Take a left, and head over the wooden footbridge across a braid of Butano Creek.

For the next 0.75 mile the trail leads along a levee through the marshland. Have the children keep a lookout for small mammals such as muskrats and raccoons, especially during the spring mating season. Also have them look for the small, tepee-like nests of muskrats beside the water. Waterfowl and shorebirds feed in the marsh and open water along the levee. Keep an eye out for different types of waterfowl, and maybe keep count of how many different types you spot. Although it is interesting to know the names of the different birds, and you can bring a bird guide with you to assist in this, it is not necessary. You can have fun just looking for different ones.

Another thing to watch for along the levee is the different plant growth as you go farther up the creek, away from the ocean. Some plants can survive in the brackish water (mixture of salt- and freshwater) closer to the ocean, while others can survive only in freshwater.

At about 0.75 mile the levee takes a sharp turn to the right, and heads back toward Pescadero Road. There is a thicker growth of tules and other marsh plants here. Look for smaller birds such as the redwing blackbird along this stretch. Discuss why there are some small trees such as willow along this stretch when there weren't before. (They live past the normal reaches of the brackish water, which willow and most other small trees can't tolerate.)

At about 1 mile the trail leaves the marsh and enters a parking lot near Pescadero Road, where there are rest rooms. Take a sharp right turn out of the parking lot to return on the trail uphill from the marsh.

Along this section of trail, which is bordered by coastal scrub, there are many more small birds. You also may see some small mammals.

The trail here also offers a better view of the marshland you have just passed through because it is somewhat higher.

At 1.5 miles you return to the trail that leads back to the parking area. Turn left and return through the coastal scrub.

24 BEAN HOLLOW BEACH TRAIL

Type	▪ Day hike
Difficulty	▪ Easy for children
Distance	▪ 2 miles, round trip
Hiking time	▪ 2 hours
Elevation gain	▪ Minimal
Hikable	▪ Year-round
Map	▪ Bean Hollow State Beach

Some of the most spectacular rock and surf scenery along the northern section of California's central coast is found along this hike. While there are no large, sandy beaches, there is a small, intimate

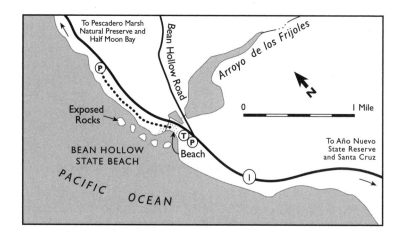

Explore the interesting rock formations that stand above the waves.

one at the southern terminus of the trail at Bean Hollow State Beach, and there are wave-battered rocks, some tide pools, and an excellent view of a harbor seal rookery along the shore. The coast along here is comprised of sandstone and an unusual rocky material known as the Pigeon Point Formation. This 65-million- to 70-million-year-old formation is a tough, erosion-resistant con- glomerate of rock and sand that extends from Pescadero Creek to Año Nuevo Point.

There are parking lots at both the north and south ends of the trail along the terraces of Bean Hollow State Park, which is located alongside CA 1, about 8 miles south of Pescadero State Park. I prefer to park at the southern end, where the small cove with Bean Hollow State Beach is located. The trail heads north along the terrace from this parking lot.

The self-guided trail leads north from the beach and climbs up on the marine terrace at about 0.25 mile. The trail leads along the edge of this terrace, which is covered by coastal scrub. Because the winds and waves along the shoreline here combine the salt spray with the air, plants that grow on the terrace must be salt-tolerant. This limits what plants can survive here.

Offshore between 0.25 mile and 0.5 mile are a number of wave-battered rocks that are covered with white material. This is guano, or excrement, from cormorants and other ocean-feeding birds that roost there. During low tide you often see large groups of these birds resting on the rocks. They frequently have their wings spread wide to dry them off after diving for fish.

Between 0.5 mile and 0.75 mile the rocks and reefs offshore are often covered with lazing harbor seals. These seals feed on fish below and then return to the exposed rocks to rest and digest their meals. Young males can frequently be seen jousting for position on the rocks. The seals are safe from sharks and any other ocean predators while they are out of the sea.

The steep cliffs between 0.75 mile and 1 mile are a good example of how each year erosion removes hundreds of acres of land from the California shoreline. Softer cliffs can erode up to 20 feet in one year, while hard ones like those at Bean Hollow may only erode 6 inches. Most of this erosion takes place during the high waves of winter storms. There are several gullies along this last section of trail where you can see how high the waves reach during the winter. Have the children guess how far the waves reach and estimate how far that is from the normal high tide mark far below.

The trail ends at 1 mile. Return to Bean Hollow Beach Cove where Bean Hollow Creek enters the ocean.

SANTA CLARA COUNTY

25 CORTE MADERA/MEADOWLARK/ ACORN TRAILS LOOP

Type ▪ Day hike
Difficulty ▪ Difficult for children
Distance ▪ 4-mile loop
Hiking time ▪ 3 hours
Elevation gain ▪ 400 feet
Hikable ▪ Year-round
Map ▪ City of Palo Alto

A small lake surrounded by tules and cattails can be found near the north end of 600-acre Arastradero Preserve, and an oak-studded ridge crosses the southern end. Between the two there are more than 6 miles of trails—formerly ranch roads—where it is easy to find peace and solitude.

Take the Page Mill Road exit off I-280. Head south to Arastradero Road and turn right. The preserve parking lot is on the north side of the road in 0.5 mile. Take the path from the parking area, across Arastradero Road to the preserve entrance.

The Corte Madera Trail follows along Arastradero Creek from

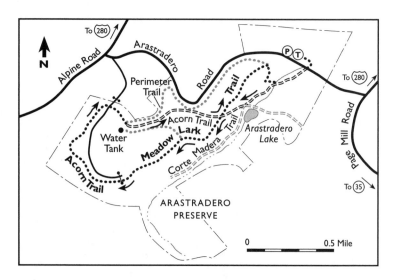

the parking lot to Arastradero Lake. The creek can be a powerful, rolling stream during winter rains, but by summer it becomes a trickle that is an inviting place for children to explore. In about 0.25 mile the trail crosses over the creek and climbs up a small hill that is covered with orange poppies and blue lupine during the spring bloom. Large oaks rise above the green grassland.

At just past 0.5 mile a gravel road crosses the Corte Madera Trail. Arastradero Lake is another 100 yards or so past the trail junction. You may want to stop at the lake, where the children can explore in the reeds and cattails that grow around the shallow edges of this small, tree-shaded lake. Redwing blackbirds and mallard ducks abound here in the spring, and mating noises can be heard from some distance away. Backtrack to the junction and take the gravel road to your left. In about 0.25 mile the road comes to the Meadowlark Trail. Take a left and begin an uphill climb. You may see red-tailed hawks or northern harriers as they patrol the grasslands for rodents and other food. Occasionally a great blue heron soars overhead on its way to the lake.

You continue across open grassland that is a carpet of brilliant wildflowers in the spring, and at just over 1 mile Meadowlark Trail crosses the Acorn Trail. Stay on Meadowlark as it continues a gentle climb to the crest of a hill. At about 1.5 miles Meadowlark Trail becomes Acorn Trail, and after you pass through a gate it becomes a gravel road.

Acorn Trail leads off to the left of the gravel road and descends past oak trees that are sprinkled over fields of wild oats that form a green carpet during the spring. Bright wildflowers are visible through the green carpet during the spring and early summer.

Open grasslands offer excellent views of the rolling hills beyond.

At just under 2 miles, near the white boundary fence, Acorn Trail takes a sharp right turn, heads into a forest, and drops down beside a little stream. This is an excellent place to stop for a rest and lunch as the children play around the creek and explore along its banks.

After eating and resting you continue down the trail until it reaches gravel road again at just under 2.5 miles. Cross the road as Acorn Trail takes a right and go through the opening in the fence as it heads uphill across a pasture.

At the water tank near 2.75 miles you take the trail to the left (both this trail and the one straight ahead are sections of the Acorn Trail) and follow the contour of a tree-shaded hillside. In the cool under the trees, ferns and horsetails grow.

By 3 miles you reach a plateau in the center of the preserve, and the Perimeter Trail leads off to the left. Stay right on Acorn Trail as it crosses a meadow. From this section of the trail there are good views of the cities along the shores of the bay.

At about 3.25 miles Acorn Trail crosses the Meadowlark Trail. Take a left on Meadowlark as it heads gently downhill. Go past the first trail junction until about 3.75 miles, where the Meadowlark Trail dead-ends at the Perimeter Trail. Take a right on the Perimeter Trail and return to the parking area.

26 BOARDWALK/CATWALK TRAILS LOOP

Type ▪	Day hike
Difficulty ▪	Easy for children
Distance ▪	1.5-mile loop
Hiking time ▪	1 hour
Elevation gain ▪	None
Hikable ▪	Year-round
Map ▪	City of Palo Alto

Visit the Lucy Evans Nature Interpretive Center in the Palo Alto Baylands Nature Preserve before beginning this hike. It stands on pilings by a levee on the edge of the marsh and has programs on bay ecology. Naturalists also conduct workshops and walks. The 120 acres of salt marsh and slough surrounding the center are a wildlife

Boardwalks make it possible to view tidelands from above.

sanctuary, and the trails and boardwalks lead you through samples of several baylands environments.

Take the Embarcadero Road exit off US 101 in Palo Alto and go east for just over 0.5 mile to the sign for the Palo Alto Baylands. Park in the lot to the left at the end of the road.

From the interpretive center, walk across the deck toward the bay and follow the boardwalk across the marsh. Some of the many salt-tolerant plants native to these marshes, such as cordgrass, pickleweed, and salt grass, grow beneath the boardwalk, and you get an excellent view of them from above.

See if you and your children can pick out what "niche" each of these plants lives in around the marsh. (Each plant that lives in salt-water marshes has a different tolerance level for salt and for the length of time it can stay submerged under the high tides. Check out your guesses at the interpretive center exhibits.)

Continue straight ahead on the boardwalk until you reach the observation platform at about 0.25 mile. From here you can look out over the mud flats and open water of the bay. Many types of shorebirds can be observed as they seek their food in the shallow water and mud. You may want to bring a bird field guide to help identify these, or you may check out the various local species at the interpretive center.

After watching the shorebirds you can return toward the interpretive center for about 200 yards on the boardwalk until you reach the catwalk that heads south over the marsh. Take a left on the catwalk, which is much narrower than the boardwalk and has no railings. Caution children that they can get wet and muddy if they

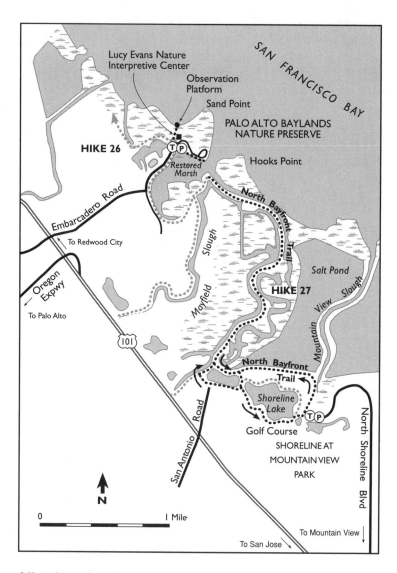

fall in here, but there is no real danger because the marsh is so shallow.

The catwalk crosses what appears from a distance to be an unbroken field of cordgrass, but close up you can see that many little streams, sloughs, and mud flats meander through it. This is an incredibly rich life zone. Marshes such as this have more living organisms than any other comparably sized plant community in the world. Counting the smallest microorganisms, there are billions of living things in each handful of mud from the marsh. These small organisms are the bottom of the food chain that extends upward to the large shorebirds and small mammals that inhabit these marshes.

The catwalk turns to the right as it passes beneath large power transmission lines at about 0.75 mile and heads overland as it circles the shore of a wide channel where several sloughs join before entering the bay.

There are several benches at the parking area where you can have lunch and look out over the bay and marsh.

27 NORTH BAYFRONT TRAIL LOOP

Type ▪	Day hike
Difficulty ▪	Moderate for children
Distance ▪	3-mile loop
Hiking time ▪	2 hours
Elevation gain ▪	None
Hikable ▪	Year-round
Map ▪	City of Mountain View
	See page 98 for Hike 27 map

Mountain View opened its Shoreline Park in 1983, and each year several million people visit there. The 7 miles of paved trails lead hikers and strollers along the bay front and through sloughs and marshes. There are several observation platforms and benches for those who wish to sit and observe. Bird watchers particularly like these. Much of the park's 544 acres are rolling hills that sit over what was once mountains of sanitary landfill.

Take the Shoreline Boulevard exit off US 101 in Mountain View, eventually head east, and continue 1 mile to the park entrance.

From the parking area, head north along the west side of Mountain View Slough toward the North Bayfront Trail. Depending on the tide, you can watch either shorebirds searching for food in the mud flats, or waterfowl diving for food in the shallow water.

At about 0.25 mile the trail takes a sharp left turn away from the slough and heads west along the edge of a salt pond on the right. This large expanse of water is a Leslie Salt Company salt-evaporator pond. Water is admitted to this and similar ponds around the bay during the summer when the bay water is at its highest salinity. San Francisco Bay is one of the few places in the country where salt is made by solar evaporation.

The small, brush-covered humps that dot the salt ponds are duck blinds. These have been passed down through family ownership for more than eighty years and are still used during the three months of duck hunting season. They are all at least 500 yards from the shore, far past the range of shotguns, so the hunters do not endanger hikers in any way.

At about 0.75 mile you can see the levee that borders Charleston Slough to the right, and a trail veers left to circle the forebay of the slough and the freshwater marsh that surrounds it. Information panels along the trail tell you about the many types of birds that feed and nest here. Continue around the forebay until the trail spur returns to the main trail. Take a right on the main trail and walk up the levee on the west side of Charleston Slough.

This levee winds through the slough and its surrounding marshes to a tip of land that juts into the bay between Hooks Point and Sand Point. There, at about 1.5 miles, you are at the bay end of the city's flood-control basin. Bird watching is excellent along this stretch of the trail. Large egrets use their long legs to carry them through the shallow waters and oozy mud as they search for small animal snacks; avocets sweep low over the marshes as they search

Keep an eye out above. You never know what's heading your way.

for a landing spot; and land birds such as meadowlarks, redwing blackbirds, sparrows, and burrowing owls use the dry land found on the small, low islands in the marsh to feed and nest. The burrowing owl is a reclusive bird that burrows into the ground to build its nest, and children like to hunt for the openings to these. During early evening you can sometimes spot the owls leaving their nests to forage for food.

This point at the end of Mayfield Slough is a good place to stop for a rest or lunch while the children keep an eye out for the many birds, and maybe an occasional muskrat or field mouse. With luck they may even see a marsh hawk dive for food.

Turn around at the point and return by the same route to the forebay. There you can take the trail to the right or the left at the golf course lake. They both wind around the lake and take you to the parking area.

28 DEER HOLLOW FARM TRAIL LOOP

Type ■ Day hike
Difficulty ■ Easy for children
Distance ■ 3-mile loop
Hiking time ■ 2 hours
Elevation gain ■ 50 feet
Hikable ■ Year-round
Map ■ Midpeninsula Regional Open Space District

A Santa Clara County park and the Midpeninsula Regional Open Space District's Rancho San Antonio Open Space Preserve join together to form a 1100-acre foothill park that consists of a wide diversity of plant communities. The valley floor has creek sides shaded by spreading oaks, and trails lead up through dry chaparral to oak/madrone forests. All of these, plus the easy accessibility of the preserve, make this one of the most popular preserves in Santa Clara County.

Take the Foothill Boulevard exit off I-280. Take an immediate right on Cristo Rey Drive on the west side of the freeway and continue

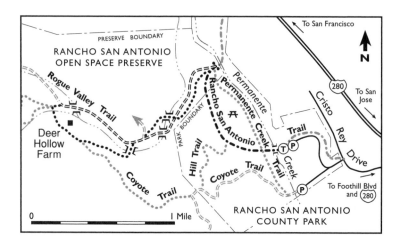

1 mile to the county park entrance. The preserve trails begin from the northwest parking lot.

Take the trail over the bridge to the north side of the parking lot and veer to the right along the creek. At about 0.25 mile you come to an area with unkempt baseball fields and some tennis courts. The creek can be reached through several openings along here, and as you pass the old handball courts, you come to a downed oak that is a favorite climbing spot for children.

Continue on the trail and just past 0.5 mile you come to a gate. Turn left here, and you have a choice of following a paved road or

Experience an old farm as you take a break in your hike.

taking a footpath. I prefer the footpath, but if you have a stroller or wheelchair you will want to take the paved road.

The footpath crosses grassland and goes through open oak forests until about 0.75 mile. There it recrosses the paved road and then a footbridge across a year-round creek. The children can explore along the banks of the creek in the summer, but it is often a roaring torrent in the winter.

The path follows alongside the road, separated by a picket fence, after it crosses the creek until just before 1 mile. There you can either turn to the right to take the road, now dirt, directly to the farm, or you can cross the road, and a footbridge on the left, to head up the side of a hill on the path. This path takes you uphill from the farm around the contour of the hill. At 1.5 miles you curve back around to enter the farm from the rear.

Children like to explore the old farm, operated by the City of Mountain View as a working reminder of the farms that were once common in Santa Clara County.

Return to the parking area by the road or the path.

29 SAN ANDREAS FAULT/ FRANCISCAN/LOST CREEK TRAILS LOOP

Type ▪	Day hike
Difficulty ▪	Moderate for children
Distance ▪	2.5-mile loop
Hiking time ▪	2 hours
Elevation gain ▪	400 feet
Hikable ▪	Year-round
Map ▪	Midpeninsula Regional Open Space District

Los Trancos Open Space Preserve is one of many open-space preserves in Santa Clara and San Mateo Counties. It contains 274 acres and more than 7 miles of trails, including the 0.6-mile loop of the San Andreas Fault interpretive earthquake trail, which cross over rolling grassland and through cool, shaded forests of oak and bay.

These weeds offer a visual delight.

Take the Page Mill Road exit off I-280 and go south for 7 miles. The preserve entrance and a small parking area are located on the north side of the road.

You begin on the San Andreas Fault Trail, which is a self-guided study trail. There are brochures available at the parking lot for this trail, and they are packed with information. This hike does not complete the circle of the study trail, however, but turns left on the Franciscan Trail Loop just before 0.25 mile.

You can look straight up the San Andreas Fault toward Crystal Springs Lake as you cross the meadow on the trail. This fault line marks the junction of two large tectonic plates, the Pacific and the North American, and movement along it causes many of the violent earth movements that have shaken the San Francisco Bay region for centuries.

The trail drops down into a woodland of massive canyon oaks at about 0.5 mile. This trail leading to the woodlands is surrounded by brilliant wildflowers in the spring and during the fall the deciduous oak and big-leaf maple add color as they turn bright gold and yellow.

Just past 0.5 mile you cross a bridge over Los Trancos Creek and climb up a short hill to an open area where the Franciscan Trail joins the Lost Creek Trail. Take a left turn and continue up a rise through the woods. At the top of the rise about 100 yards past the junction, and at about 0.75 mile, the trail takes a sharp left and follows a ridge down into the canyon of Los Trancos Creek.

As you descend along the ridge, large firs begin to rise high above the oak, and you can see them across the canyon as you reach the creek. Wild rose and currant add color to the hillsides with their pink blossoms in the spring, and the blossoms of false Solomon's seal, star flower, and trillium join them. Ferns and mosses are thick along the banks and on the boulders of the creek.

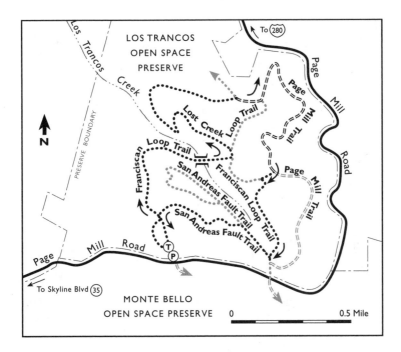

This is a good place to stop for a rest and to let the children explore along the creek.

At about 1 mile the trail veers away from the narrow gorge of the creek and follows alongside a tributary where tremendous oaks and bays shade the hillside. It soon leaves the tributary and begins a climb back to the ridge, joining with Page Mill Trail at about 1.25 miles.

Turn right on Page Mill Trail, and then right again on Lost Creek Trail at about 1.5 miles. This takes you back to the flat and the junction of Lost Creek and Franciscan Trails. Take the Franciscan Trail to the left out of the flat as it slowly descends into a group of large bay trees. The trail circles around a small hill and outcroppings of limestone that the children can climb on. Some of the huge oaks in the area have limbs that probably broke off in the violent 1906 earthquake.

The trail climbs gradually into open grassland by about 2 miles. Bright patches of wildflower blooms cover the green hillsides here in the spring.

At about 2.25 miles take the trail to the right. This leads to the San Andreas Fault Trail. At the junction with the Franciscan Trail, take the left fork and head back to the parking area.

30 STEVENS CREEK NATURE TRAIL

Type ■ Day hike
Difficulty ■ Difficult for children
Distance ■ 3-mile loop
Hiking time ■ 3 hours
Elevation gain ■ 450 feet
Hikable ■ Year-round
Map ■ Midpeninsula Regional Open Space District

The various units of Midpeninsula Regional Open Space District and the county park system in this area total more than 4500 acres. These cover most of Stevens Creek Canyon between Page Mill Road and Saratoga Gap and from Skyline Boulevard to Monte Bello Ridge. This large tract of near-wilderness woodlands,

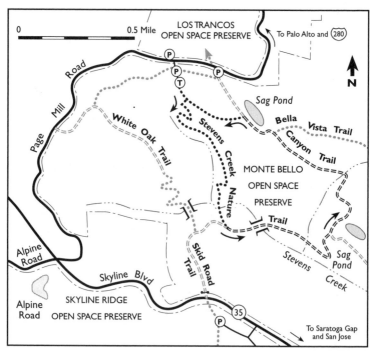

grasslands, and cool, damp canyons where creeks run year-round is located near major population centers on the peninsula. Monte Bello Open Space Preserve, one of the first preserves acquired by the Midpeninsula Regional Open Space District, covers almost 2700 acres and includes the upper reaches of Stevens Creek.

Take the Page Mill Road exit off I-280 and continue 7 miles south on Page Mill Road. Park in the parking lot at the preserve entrance on the south side of the road just past the Los Trancos Open Space Preserve entrance on the opposite side of the road.

From the parking lot take the nature trail straight ahead as it begins a steady descent downhill toward a mixed evergreen forest. The trail crosses open grassland for the first 0.25 mile, and then takes a sharp left turn into the woods.

Both deer and coyotes like the zone where the forest meets the grassland, and you may see signs of them if you look closely. They prefer early morning and late evening for their outings into the open meadows, but you may be able to spot some deer droppings or coyote scat. You may also find some tracks if there has been a recent rain.

From 0.25 mile to 0.5 mile the self-guided trail leads by dead trees that are teeming with life such as woodpeckers, termites, bark beetles, and fungi of various kinds. Just past 0.5 mile there is an area where the hillside slid during the 1983 storms, and the steep scarp where the sliding earth carried large trees is unmistakable.

Just before 1 mile the trail crosses a tributary of Stevens Creek by bridge. The often-overflowing stream has formed a small flat area where it enters Stevens Creek. This is a good place for the children to explore the creek bed. Insects, and birds that feed on them, such as flycatchers, are abundant here, and tracks of deer, raccoons, skunks, and even an occasional bobcat can often be found in the mud near the creek.

The trail begins a short climb after it crosses the bridge and veers right. During high water you may want to turn around at the bridge and return by the trail you came on, for there are several spots ahead where you must ford the creek. If the creek is low at the bridge there should be no problem ahead, although the trail may be slippery if there has been recent rain.

Between 1 mile and 1.5 miles the trail follows Stevens Creek upstream. You pass by an area with a thick understory of ferns, berries, honeysuckles, and nettles. These crowd along the creek banks as horsetails and coltsfoot grow in the streambed itself.

When the water level goes down, explore what's left high and dry.

At about 1.5 miles the stream has undercut the creek bank and exposed the roots of some large trees. These are likely to fall in the near future as large winter storms bring floodwaters. Have the children guess how the large boulders in the stream got there, and use their size to show the strength of the roaring waters of winter. You must ford the creek here because all of the bridges that have been built across the creek have washed out.

As the trail begins a steep climb uphill at 1.5 miles, there are some terraces where ladybugs love to congregate. Thousands of them winter here in dense clusters on grass stems and tree trunks. They stay near water, but above the winter floods. As the weather warms in the spring the ladybugs become extremely active and mate. The eggs hatch in April, and the larvae eat aphids for about three weeks before pupating.

As the trail climbs up the hill, you can see large fir stumps that indicate there was a heavy stand of fir here like the one still standing across the creek.

As the trail joins an old skid road it becomes Canyon Trail. The old road was made by loggers about 100 years ago when they logged the firs that stood on the hillside. Bay, madrone, tanoak, and an understory of hazelnuts and ferns share the hillsides with the fir.

The exposed rock on the side of the roadcut at between 1.5 and 2 miles is a bluish-gray serpentine. This is California's state rock, and it was formed by compression along the fault lines that run through the mountains.

At about 2.5 miles a creek flows out of the limestone bedrock uphill from the road. If the children examine the rocks, leaves, and twigs along this creek, they will find that they appear to be fossilized. This is because the hard granular limestone that has precipitated out of the stream water as it flows downstream has hardened as it coated all the items in the creek. This precipitation occurs only in the warm water of summer. As you pass the stream and look downhill, you can see where the fault zone lies below the road. There is an unusual pattern of ridges and valleys that was formed as the San Andreas Fault broke into multiple fault lines here.

Just past 2.5 miles there is a sag pond with heavy growth of tules and cattails around its edges. This shallow pond was formed at a curve in the fault where gradual movement has forced the edges of the fault line apart, forming a sag in the line where water can collect. This sag pond is fed by springs from along Monte Bello Ridge.

Have the children guess why there is so much growth in the pond. Then discuss how plants die, leaving material that decays and forms sediment that gradually fills in the sag. Plants grow in the sediment, and slowly the pond fills. This gradual replacement is part of the normal progression that occurs in ponds of all types.

The trail takes off to the left about 100 yards past the pond and heads uphill through open grassland back to the parking area.

31 HICKORY OAK RIDGE TRAIL LOOP

Type ▪	Day hike
Difficulty ▪	Easy for children
Distance ▪	2 miles, round trip
Hiking time ▪	1 hour
Elevation gain ▪	100 feet
Hikable ▪	Year-round
Map ▪	Midpeninsula Regional Open Space District

Looking west from Skyline Boulevard, you will see spectacular views of Big Basin Redwoods State Park in Santa Cruz County and of Butano Ridge. The 1011 acres of Long Ridge Open Space Preserve are located on the slope to the west of Skyline Boulevard, and the 10 miles of trails that traverse the preserve offer

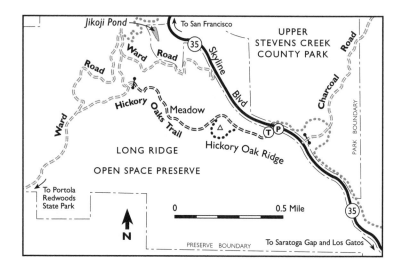

plenty of these vistas as they cross grasslands interspersed with oak/madrone/Douglas-fir forests. Near the southern end of the preserve, Hickory Oak Ridge is home to an excellent hickory oak (also known as canyon oak) forest.

Take Skyline Boulevard south from Page Mill Road for just less than 5 miles (2 miles past the main entrance and parking area for Long Ridge Open Space Preserve) to the small parking area for the Hickory Oak Ridge Area. Park on the west side of the road near the hikers' stile.

Follow the old ranch road as you pass through the hikers' stile, and head through the woods. The road turns right after about 100 yards, where wide-canopied hickory oaks stand tall over the road. These oaks, also know as canyon or maul oak, have massive trunks, some more than 5 feet in diameter, and their large horizontal limbs are often twisted into grotesque shapes. Have the children look at the limbs and massive trunks and imagine them as characters from some book, maybe "ents" from The *Lord of the Rings* trilogy. The fine-grained hardwood of these trees was used for making farm implements during the 1800s.

At about 0.5 mile, the trail passes out of the trees and into an open meadow rimmed with trees and filled with rock outcroppings. This meadow is full of bright wildflower blooms in the spring, and the view of Oil Creek from the top of the hill is well worth the little side trip.

As you return to the road, you again walk through an oak forest until about 0.75 mile, when you come to open grassland. The road

Follow the leader

climbs over rolling hills until 1 mile, when you reach a gate that marks the end of the trail.

Return by the same route. You may wish to climb back to the top of the first meadow for a picnic before heading for the parking area.

32 LOOKOUT TRAIL

Type ■	Day hike
Difficulty ■	Easy for children
Distance ■	1.5 miles, round trip
Hiking time ■	1 hour
Elevation gain ■	440 feet
Hikable ■	Year-round
Map ■	Santa Clara County Park

Stevens Creek County Park sits among several Midpeninsula Regional Open Space District preserves. It encompasses a large foothill canyon that is the site of Stevens Creek Reservoir, and the steep hillsides of the canyon are covered with oak woodlands and open grasslands. Trails lead around the reservoir, along the creek above the reservoir, and to the ridges above the canyon.

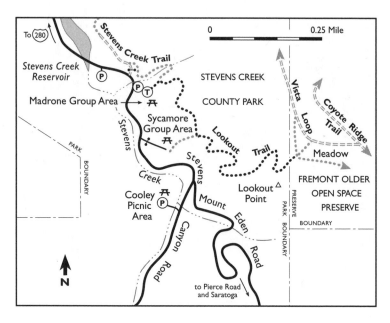

Take the Foothill Boulevard exit off I-280 south until it becomes Stevens Canyon Road. About 2 miles from the freeway, the north entrance to the park is on the left. The visitor center and several trailheads are located here. The visitor center is well designed and worth a stop, but the trailhead for this hike is located about 1.5 miles farther along on Stevens Canyon Road, which runs through the park before its intersection with Mount Eden Road. Take the trail that leads out of Picnic Area No. 2.

The trailhead for Lookout Trail is behind the picnic area rest rooms. It crosses the low ridge that separates Picnic Area No. 2 from the Sycamore Picnic Area, and after about 200 yards a side trail from the Sycamore Picnic Area comes up a small ravine to the right and joins with the Lookout Trail.

Continue straight ahead on the Lookout Trail as it climbs a steep slope. The trail is shaded from the hot, midday sun here as a series of switchbacks leads through an oak and toyon forest. The slopes are an emerald green, and wild irises, ferns, and wild roses add color here after the winter rains. During the spring have the children look for small crawling animals among the lush ground growth. They should be able to find several types of caterpillars and many beetles. The toyon's bright red berries stand out in the fall and winter.

At about 0.5 mile you reach the top of the first ridge. From there

Where there are winter waterfalls there is fall climbing.

you can look south over the Mount Eden Trail. Continue on uphill to the top of 1000-foot Lookout Point at 0.75 mile. As you reach the point, continue through the stile that leads out of the county park into the adjoining preserve. From there you have good views of a canyon to the west and the Fremont Older Preserve to the east.

As you return by the same trail, stop along the ridge where you can overlook the meadow below and have lunch. Horseback riders often canter across the rolling hills and trails.

33 SEVEN SPRINGS TRAIL LOOP

Type ■	Day hike
Difficulty ■	Difficult for children
Distance ■	3-mile loop
Hiking time ■	2 hours
Elevation gain ■	860 feet
Hikable ■	Year-round
Map ■	Midpeninsula Regional Open Space District

Fremont Older Open Space Preserve, on the edges of urban development, offers 734 acres and a variety of hiking experiences. Its open hayfields, 900-foot-high Hunters Point, and Seven Springs Canyon all are popular with hikers, and to the west of the park the oak- and chaparral-covered slopes drop steeply down to Stevens Canyon.

Take the CA 85 exit off I-280 and continue south to Stevens Creek Boulevard. Turn left on Stevens Creek, and then right on Stelling Road. Go 2 miles on Stelling to Prospect Road. Turn right on

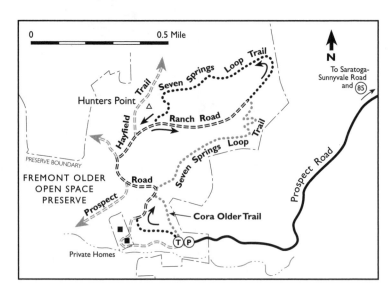

Prospect and continue for just over 1 mile to the preserve parking area.

Follow the road along the creek out of the parking area. This leads you through an oak and bay forest. At the first bend, at about 100 yards, take the marked hikers' trail off to the right. This trail continues to follow the creek until it dead-ends at the ranch road. Take a right on the road and the trail winds uphill, with open fields on both sides. In the spring the dark trunks of the old orchard trees stand out against the bright green grass.

At just over 0.5 mile the road reaches a saddle in the ridge and splits. Take the trail to the right. From here the trail follows along the ridge toward Hunters Point and the Seven Springs area.

Just as you come to the hilltop apricot orchard at about 1 mile, where the trail leads off to the left to Hunters Point, the Seven Springs Trail Loop turns right and heads downhill. There is poison oak on both sides of the old ranch road as it winds down to a lower canyon, where many springs seep from the slopes down to the canyon floor.

CAUTION

An old walnut orchard and a clump of bay trees thrive at the bottom of the canyon; this is an excellent place to stop for a picnic and let the children explore the many holes and knots in the old walnut trees. Many of these holes and crevices are home to insects and small birds, and some of the larger holes even hold enough water for small plants and animals to live in.

Lonely oaks offer some shade.

At about 1.5 miles the trail reaches the preserve boundary and turns north. It then begins to climb up the side of the hill toward Hunters Point.

At about 1.75 miles you come to a hilltop that is encircled with large oak trees. Just beyond this hilltop is a small apricot orchard. A steep climb of several hundred yards off the trail brings you to Hunters Point, where you can view the entire Santa Clara Valley.

Return on the road downhill to the parking area.

SKYLINE/SUMMIT ROCK LOOP/ BONJETTI CREEK TRAILS LOOP

Type ■	Day hike
Difficulty ■	Easy to moderate for children
Distance ■	1.5-mile loop; side trip to knoll, 1.25 miles
Hiking time ■	1 to 2 hours
Elevation gain ■	400 feet
Hikable ■	Year-round
Map ■	Santa Clara County Park

This hike first leads you to the top of a rock outcropping near the west boundary of Sanborn-Skyline County Park and then down into Bonjetti Creek Canyon. This is one of several wild canyons that can be found on the eastern slope of the Santa Cruz Mountains in Sanborn-Skyline County Park. This cool, deep canyon is an ideal summer hike when the inland areas are reaching temperatures toward 90 degrees Fahrenheit.

This trail does not begin on the east side of the park where the main entrance is, but from the western boundary of the park. From the intersection of CA 35 and CA 9, go southeast on CA 35 (Skyline Boulevard) for 1.5 miles to a turnout on the east side of the highway. Park there.

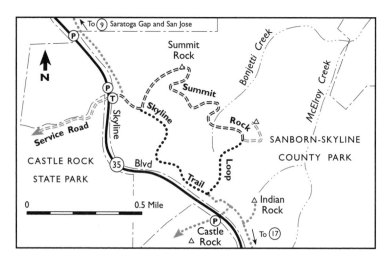

Begin the hike by heading to your right on the old Summit Road inside the park: this is the Skyline Trail. Follow it through a fir, oak, and madrone forest that is typical of those found on many of the ridges in the Santa Cruz Mountains. Muted sunlight filters through the canopy of the tall trees to a pale green growth of ferns and low-growing shrubs such as wild rose and thimbleberry.

At about 0.5 mile a well-worn path leads off to the left to Summit Rock. This large sandstone outcropping rises only about 20 feet above the ridge, but its sloped side drops off quite steeply, and for a surprisingly long way. Children

Nature's sculptures are stunning.

like to climb to the top, and this is quite easy because many holes have been eroded in the sides. Make sure they are aware of the drop-off, however, if they do climb to the top.

After a side trip to Summit Rock, return to Skyline Trail, turn left, and then take the first trail off to the left. This is the Summit Rock Trail Loop, and it leads down into Bonjetti Creek Canyon, one of many wild canyons in the Santa Cruz Mountains.

The trail follows an old wagon road across sloping meadows (which are brilliant with wildflower blooms during the spring), and into a fir forest. Some of the older trees here tower above all else and are up to 8 feet in diameter at the base.

At about 1 mile the trail comes out of the forest as it rounds a ridge and enters a slope that leads down to Bonjetti Creek. It passes along a flat where an apple orchard is the only sign left of a long-abandoned homestead. There are also some young redwoods that rise up to 100 feet along here.

You can take a side trip at about 1.25 miles by turning left on a lightly used trail at the sign "To Skyline Trail." The path leads through a corner of the orchard and then widens into an old road that takes an easy 0.25-mile climb through chaparral to the peak of a 2800-foot knoll. Oak trees now cover the top of the knoll, but the flat area was probably the site of an old home at one time.

Return to the apple orchard and take a left on the Summit Rock Trail Loop. This section of the trail is cool and shaded. At about 1.5 miles you climb a narrow ledge between Bonjetti Creek, which cascades over moss-covered rocks at high water, and a waterfall spilling over a large boulder on the other side. During the winter and spring children like the excitement and exhilaration of the sound of water crashing down over the moss-covered rocks. During the summer the flow becomes less forceful, but this gives children an opportunity to explore around the rocks where the water has excavated small ponds.

The trail rejoins the Skyline Trail at about 1.75 miles. Turn right on the Skyline Trail and head north back toward the parking area. The trail crosses a flat ridgetop, where you can hear the sounds of the highway, and passes through a fir forest before you come to the junction of the Summit Rock Trail Loop at 2 miles.

Return to the parking area by the Skyline Trail.

35 SENATOR MINE/GUADALUPE/ MINE HILLS TRAILS LOOP

Type ▪	Day hike
Difficulty ▪	Difficult for children
Distance ▪	4-mile loop
Hiking time ▪	2.5 hours
Elevation gain ▪	720 feet
Hikable ▪	Year-round
Map ▪	Santa Clara County Park

The site of Almaden Quicksilver Park along the 6-mile-long Los Capitancillos Ridge was once the most productive quicksilver (mercury) mine in the world. Now 25 miles of trails cross the more than 3500 acres of the park, where busy mines and 500 homes sat during the heyday of New Almaden. The mines operated from 1845 to 1926, and for a short period again during World War II. Today little remains to be seen of that era. Many of the trails across the park follow the old roads used during the mining days. Easy walks and strenuous hikes quickly take hikers away from the hubbub of urban Santa Clara County to secluded

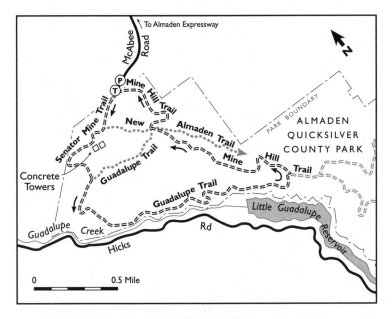

woods and panoramic views of the Santa Cruz Mountains.

There are three entrances to the park, but for this hike take the Camden Avenue exit off the Almaden Expressway and head southwest to McAbee Road. Turn west on McAbee Road and continue to the end. Park alongside the road.

Head out on the service road as it follows a creek to the Senator Mine area. The Mine Hill Trail turns to the left after about 200 yards, but continue on the service road, which becomes the Senator Mine Trail.

The canyon widens and you approach two high concrete towers at about 0.5 mile. They were part of the furnace plant, and are left from the days when the mines in the park were producing large amounts of mercury. This mine was worked until the 1920s, and a plaque by the towers tells about the processes they used at the plant to extract mercury from the cinnabar.

The trail climbs along a flat of open grassland and curves up a tree-covered canyon before it ends at a saddle at about 0.75 mile. There it joins the Guadalupe Trail. If you take the left here, you will return to the parking area for a 1.5-mile loop as you follow along a ridge. There are several good picnic spots at the saddle if you want to return to your car after eating.

Take the right if you wish to continue the longer hike, and head

Use these as stepping-stones to adventure.

downhill toward Guadalupe Creek. Mount Umunhum, at 3500 feet one of the highest peaks in the Santa Cruz Mountains, can be seen as you head down the trail. The multistoried building on its top helps you easily identify this peak. Have the children guess what the building may have been used for. (It was a military installation.)

By 1 mile you can see Guadalupe Creek running below, and the grass-covered hillsides beside the trail have several species of lilies blooming among the high grasses during the spring and early summer.

The trail comes close to the creek by 1.5 miles, but you cannot explore along the banks here because the creek is outside the park boundaries. The meadows here are a brilliant carpet of wildflower blooms in the spring, however, and broad-canopied oaks offer intermittent shade along the park boundary.

By 1.75 miles the trail turns away from the creek and climbs level with Guadalupe Dam, which retains the waters of the Little Guadalupe Reservoir as it stretches 1.5 miles upstream. Although the waters of the reservoir are inviting, the sides of the canyon are so steep that there is little access to the water's edge.

As the trail climbs away from the reservoir at just under 2 miles, there is a place to stop for a rest or a picnic under some oak trees. You can look out over the reservoir as you rest.

At about 2.25 miles the trail turns away from the reservoir and dead-ends at the Mine Hill Trail at a saddle. This is a good place to stop for a rest and a picnic if you didn't stop above the reservoir.

Take a left on Mine Hill Trail and head back through open meadows and groves of oak to the park entrance. Wildflowers abound along this stretch of the trail during the spring and early summer. Have the children keep track of how many different types of wildflowers they spot as they walk along the trail.

36 HIDDEN SPRINGS/COYOTE PEAK/RIDGE TRAILS LOOP

Type:	▪ Day hike
Difficulty	▪ Moderate for children
Distance	▪ 3-mile loop
Hiking time	▪ 2 hours
Elevation gain	▪ 600 feet
Hikable	▪ Year-round
Map	▪ Santa Clara County Park

Coyote Peak, at 1155 feet, stands sentinel over the 1600 acres of Santa Teresa Park. A golf course and an archery range occupy much of the park's low-lying area, and trails crisscross grasslands, rock outcroppings, and forested ravines of the hills around Coyote Peak. The grasslands are a sea of bright-colored wildflowers in the spring, and some bloom even as late as fall, when the small white flowers of tarweed stand out in the brown grasses. There was some mining in the park during the 1800s, but the mines were not very productive. Tailings, or rocks and soil removed from the underground mines, from the Bernal Mine can still be seen on some hillsides.

Take the Bernal Road exit off US 101 and continue south 2.5 miles until you reach the center of the park. Turn left at the first road past the Girls' Ranch, and continue to the picnic area and parking lot.

Take a right turn on the Hidden Springs Trail out of the Pueblo Group Area. The trail crosses open grasslands that have profuse blooms of wildflowers during the spring and early summer, and, as it rounds a hill, crosses a year-round stream at about 0.25 mile.

The Ridge Trail enters from the left, but keep right on the Hidden Springs Trail. Continue uphill past a small, spring-fed pond at about 0.5 mile.

At about 0.75 mile you reach a high saddle, and the Coyote Peak Trail leads off to the right. Take it and head for the top of 1155-foot Coyote Peak. You reach the peak at about 1.25 miles and, from the level surface that was graded off for a military communications installation during World War II, you have a commanding view of the Santa Clara Valley and mountain ranges to the east, south, and west.

While you are at the peak have the children look overhead to see if they can distinguish the vultures from the red-tailed hawks that are generally soaring above. The vultures have a characteristic

There's always something interesting along a trail.

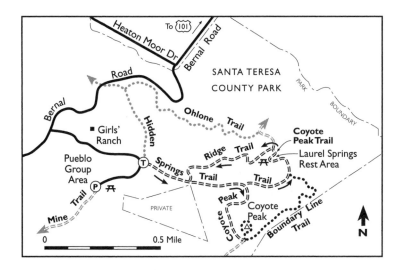

V-shape to their wings as they soar, while the red-tailed hawks keep their wings quite level.

You can use either the Boundary Line Trail or the Coyote Peak Trail on your return, but I prefer the Coyote Peak Trail because the other is steep and gravelly. If you do use the Boundary Line Trail, you will connect with the Hidden Springs Trail at about 1.5 miles. Turn right and the Laurel Springs Rest Area is beside the trail after about 100 yards.

If you return on the Coyote Peak Trail, take a right (east) at the first junction, and continue on the Coyote Peak Trail as it descends through chaparral and passes an occasional large tree. At about 1.5 miles the Boundary Line Trail enters from the right. Stay on the Coyote Peak Trail for about 100 yards to the Laurel Springs Rest Area. Turn left into the rest area, where huge old bay trees (also known as laurel trees) form a canopy over picnic tables and a horse-tying rack. A nearby spring feeds a creek that runs all year except in years that are extremely dry. A luxurious growth of elderberry and fern sprout from this wet area.

Children love to play on the large trunks of several old bay trees that have fallen by the trail. Have them look at the many sprouts coming up from both the roots and the trunk. Compare this method of regeneration with that of the redwood, which also sprouts from old stumps and roots.

After a rest stop take the Ridge Trail out of the rest area as it makes a steep climb uphill. At about 1.75 miles it makes several sharp turns, and then begins a series of ups and downs. These take you through open grassland that is full of brilliant blooms during the springtime, and under old oaks where there is welcome relief on hot summer days. The Ridge Trail joins the Hidden Springs Trail at about 2 miles. Take a right onto the Hidden Springs Trail and continue back to the Pueblo Group Area as the trail makes a gentle descent over rolling hills.

37 SWANSON CREEK NATURE TRAIL LOOP

Type ▪	Day hike
Difficulty ▪	Moderate for children
Distance ▪	3-mile loop
Hiking time ▪	2 hours
Elevation gain ▪	600 feet
Hikable ▪	Year-round
Map ▪	Santa Clara County Park

The drive to Uvas Canyon Park is one of the most colorful in Santa Clara County during the spring wildflower bloom. The trip leads you down backcountry roads through open grasslands and oak woodlands that cover rolling hills. Uvas Creek runs alongside Croy Road on the last leg of the drive, and it is lined the whole way with alders, maples, and redwoods. The 1100 acres of the park are typical of the steep, rugged terrain found in the Santa Cruz Mountains, and three live creeks have cut deep canyons as they flow down from Skyline Ridge. The deep canyons are cool, moist, and heavily forested, but the south-facing, sun-drenched slopes are covered with chaparral. The creeks fall in cascades over moss-covered boulders after heavy winter rains, and spring is a favorite time for many to visit the park.

Take the Bernal Road exit off US 101 and head west for 1 mile to Santa Teresa Boulevard. Turn left on Santa Teresa and continue 3 miles to Bailey Avenue. Turn right on Bailey and drive until it dead-ends at McKean Road. Go left on McKean and continue as it becomes Uvas Road. Continue south past Chesbro Reservoir County Park on the left. About 2 miles past Chesbro Reservoir County

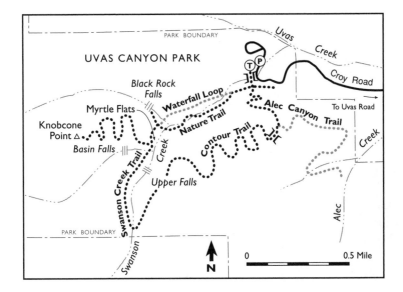

Park, turn right on Croy Road. Continue on Croy Road to the end and the park entrance. Park at the Black Oak Youth Group Area.

This hike starts along Swanson Creek Nature Trail as it heads upstream from the picnic area. Have the children decide which way to go after you tell them to head upstream. If they don't know which way is upstream, have them drop a stick or leaf in the stream to see which way it will float. Tell them to take the opposite direction.

At about 0.25 mile you cross to the north side of the creek over a bridge that was rebuilt after a devastating storm in 1986. Have the children imagine how high and strong the flow of the creek must have been to take out the bridge.

After about 100 yards take the stairway to your left, cross back over the creek, and reach the Nature Trail. This narrow footpath follows closely along the creek. This is a self-guided trail (a ranger can give you a brochure) that marks native trees and shrubs. Wide-spreading tanoak, maple, and alder provide shade for the trail and the cool-loving plants such as fern and moss that grow on the canyon banks along the creek. This creek often roars as it rushes over the rocky bottom.

The trail crosses over the creek several times before it rejoins the Swanson Creek Nature Trail, as well as several others, at about 0.5 mile. A tributary of Swanson Creek enters at this junction, and a short hike of about 100 yards up the trail straight across from the

What might be living in this knothole?

Nature Trail leads you to Black Rock Falls. There the water cascades over large, dark boulders that give the falls its name. The Myrtle Flats Rest Area is also located at this junction. (Myrtle is another of the many names given to the California bay trees that grow here, as well as another name for the sprawling ground cover also known as periwinkle.)

Return to the junction and take the Swanson Creek Trail left up toward Myrtle Flats. A trail to Knobcone Point leads off to the right here and goes about 0.25 mile up to a hill where a homestead once stood. Take this interesting side trip if your group has energy to spare.

You pass by several signs of former habitation as you head toward Myrtle Flats. Myrtle (or periwinkle), with its bright blue flowers, has covered the hillside, and there is an old cement dam on the creek. A picnic table sits on a terrace above the dam.

At 1 mile there is a wide clearing in the forest, and a spur trail leads off to the right along another tributary of Swanson Creek. Turn up this trail for about 100 yards to Basin Falls, which drops into a small, oval pool among the rocks. Children like to wade and explore here if the falls aren't falling too powerfully. Have them remove their shoes and socks if they decide to wade, for you don't want to have blisters from wet socks.

Return to the main trail and turn right. Almost immediately to the left on the main stream of Swanson Creek is Upper Falls. Just above the falls on the creek there is a large jumble of boulders and fallen trees. Have the children discuss how this jumble may have occurred. (It was left by the violent turbulence of the 1986 floodwaters.)

Walk around the jumble of boulders and logs as the Swanson Creek Trail continues upstream. At about 1.25 miles the trail veers to the left and crosses over the creek. There is no bridge here, so you must hop across the rocks and boulders and climb the opposite bank.

The trail is called the Contour Trail, and it takes a sharp left turn as it heads out to a broad ridge that climbs gently through an oak forest. Knobcone pines grow among the young oaks here, which indicates that there was a fire along the slope a number of years ago. Knobcone is one of several types of pine whose seeds sprout only after they have been exposed to the extreme heat of a fire. This, along with the young oaks in the area, supports the idea of a recent fire.

At about 1.5 miles the trail leads down into cool ravines where Douglas-firs provide shade for the green understory along several small streams. Gray squirrels, chickaree squirrels, and Stellar's jays all can be found here. Most often they can be heard scolding you as intruders into their realm.

At about 2 miles you cross the last ravine along the trail on a wooden bridge built by a troop of Eagle Scouts.

The Contour Trail dead-ends into the Alec Canyon Trail at about 2.5 miles. A right turn here takes you on a 0.5-mile side trip to 1520-foot Manzanita Point and Triple Falls.

A left takes you back to the parking lot at about 3 miles.

38 BANKS/BLACKHAWK CANYONS LOOP

Type ▪ Day hike
Difficulty ▪ Moderate for children
Distance ▪ 2-mile loop
Hiking time ▪ 2 hours
Elevation gain ▪ 420 feet
Hikable ▪ Year-round
Map ▪ Santa Clara County Park

Fishing in Sprig Lake, picnicking at a 3093-acre mountaintop retreat of a nineteenth-century cattle baron, and hiking on 18 miles of trails through the canyons and up the ridges of Mount Madonna Park are all activities your family can enjoy here. Mount Madonna rises to 1897 feet as the high point of the southern

Buckeye covers the hillsides during spring bloom.

Santa Cruz Mountains and offers panoramic views over Monterey Bay and the plains of the Pajaro and Salinas Rivers to the south and the Santa Clara Valley to the east. On exceptionally clear days the Santa Lucia Mountains can be seen to the south and the Diablo Range to the east. Streams roar down the steep canyons in the park over boulders, logs, and whole trees after heavy winter rains. And in the spring the wildflowers stand out brightly against the emerald of the grass-covered hillsides. Both large and small animal life is abundant here year-round.

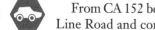

From CA 152 between Gilroy and Watsonville, turn north on Pole Line Road and continue to the park entrance and headquarters.

Head out west from the park headquarters on the service road. After about 200 yards the Blue Springs Trail leads off to the left. Take it and head through a thick growth of chaparral with an occasional knobcone pine rising high above the manzanita and ceanothus. This area has abundant blooms from early spring, when clumps of the manzanita's small, bell-shaped flowers hang from the ends of the stiff branches, through the summer, when yellow bush poppies rise through the brush of the chaparral.

The trail stays east of Pole Line Road as it goes downhill, and at a little less than 0.5 mile you come to the junction of the Blue Springs and Redwood Trails. Take a right on the Redwood Trail, which crosses Pole Line Road after about 100 yards, and head downhill on a narrow, shaded footpath. The trail continues a gentle descent toward the head of Banks Canyon through a redwood forest.

Just before 1 mile the trail crosses the head of the canyon and

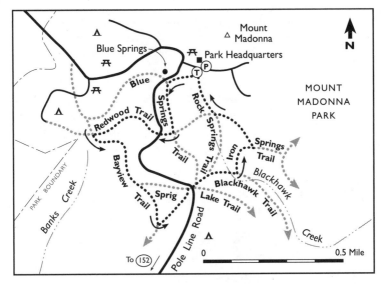

dips down toward a creek. As it passes the creek it rises out of the
canyon and joins the Bayview Trail at just past 1 mile. Take a left
on Bayview Trail. You get a view of Monterey Bay through an opening in the forest here if the summer fogs haven't come in to hang
over the Santa Cruz Mountains. If the fog is in, you will likely feel
drops of condensed fog drip from the limbs of the redwoods as it
falls to the ground. Redwoods can gather as much as 10 inches of
water a year from fog, and this helps sustain them through the long,
dry summers of the California coast.

The Bayview Trail descends into Banks Canyon and climbs back
out on several switchbacks. At just under 1.5 miles Sprig Lake Trail
leads off to the right and takes you to a trail junction along Pole
Line Road. If you continue straight on the Bayview Trail, however,
you will have an outstanding view of the Pajaro Valley and the Santa
Lucia Mountains.

After another 200 yards take a sharp left turn to head back
uphill on a horse trail to the trail junction on Pole Line Road. This
junction is at the beginning of Blackhawk Canyon, which is drained
by Blackhawk Creek. Three trails lead down Blackhawk Canyon
from the junction, and the two left trails lead back to the park headquarters. Take the broad, well-marked Blackhawk Trail as it heads
down the east side of the canyon beside the creek. Just after 1.5
miles the Iron Springs Trail leads off to the left. Make the sharp
left turn and keep along the slope.

Have the children try to guess what causes the rust-colored soil to the left of the trail. (The water seeping from Iron Springs contains vast amounts of iron, and some of the iron is deposited in the soil as the water seeps through.)

The Iron Springs Trail joins the Redwood Trail in about 200 yards. Take a sharp left turn onto the Redwood Trail as it heads uphill, and after another 200 yards take a right on the Rock Springs Trail, which leads you back to the park headquarters. If the office is open you can see exhibits on Mount Madonna's natural history.

39 SPRINGS TRAIL TO LION SPRING

Type ▪	Day hike
Difficulty ▪	Easy for children
Distance ▪	2.4 miles, round trip
Hiking time ▪	2 hour
Elevation gain ▪	340 feet
Hikable ▪	Year-round
Map ▪	California State Park

Henry W. Coe State Park is the largest mountain park in the South Bay, with more than 80,000 acres of ridges, deep canyons, and upland meadows, and 100 miles of trails. The elevations in the park range from sea level to more than 3500 feet, and large parts of the park have been classified as wilderness. Almost every ecological zone in the Coast Range can be found in the park. Oak woodlands, grasslands, coniferous forests, and riparian plant communities are typical here. Spring wildflower displays are found throughout the park, and are exceptional on Pine Ridge, in Miller Field, and in many of the remote wilderness areas. The giant manzanita found on the western ridges in the park is an unusual plant species, and the stands of ponderosa pine found in several sections of the park are very unusual in the Coast Range. Mountain lions and bobcats are seldom seen, but are known to inhabit the park's wilder regions. Wild pigs are abundant, as are deer, fox, rabbit, and squirrel. Golden eagles can often be seen soaring above it all. Some of the largest blue schist blocks found in California

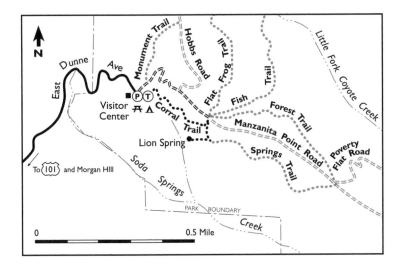

are located in the southeastern section of the park. Because the schist is more resistant to erosion than the surrounding sedimentary material, blocks as much as a half-mile across stand out prominently on hillsides and slopes. These are known as "knockers." Near the park headquarters there is also a well-preserved marine sediment layer with tiny marine fossils.

Take the East Dunne Avenue exit off US 101 near Morgan Hill and go 18 miles to the park entrance.

Take the trail downhill near the cattle-loading chute across from the visitor center. The trail heads downhill behind the barn. Take the Corral Trail toward Manzanita Point for 0.25 mile. The trail parallels a service road along this section as it passes through open grassland with large black oaks. These oaks have large, dark-green leaves with deep lobes and sharp points that turn yellow with a tinge of red in the fall.

The trail follows the gentle contour of the hillsides through these scattered oaks, then comes to a large flat area. The Corral Trail becomes the Springs Trail here, and heads off to the right. To the left is the Fish Trail. Take the Madrone Springs Trail to the right as it passes through a forest of digger and ponderosa pine, with some scattered oaks.

Within 100 yards, the trail enters another clearing. Stay on the trail for about 50 feet into the clearing, and then, at 0.3 mile, look for a little-used trail to the right. This trail leads you off the main trail to the Lion Spring campsite. The chemical toilet at the campsite

On a foggy morning you never know what you'll run into.

also serves as an indicator of the camp location if you can't locate the trail. The campsite is a good spot for a picnic if no one is camped there.

Children like to explore around the outcropping of large boulders near the campsite, and Lion Spring is located below it. The spring was originally developed as a source of water for ranch cattle, and children who lived on the ranch spent hot summer afternoons at the cool site. Supposedly they sometimes saw a mountain lion atop the boulders above the spring, but today few hikers are lucky enough to see this elusive inhabitant of the park.

Return to the Springs Trail. If you want to take a longer hike, turn to your right and head east on this trail to visit some of the 100 or more springs located in the park. Otherwise take a left and return to the Fish Trail junction. Stay to the left to return on the Corral Trail.

SAN FELIPE/BARN/HOTEL TRAILS LOOP

Type ▪ Day hike
Difficulty ▪ Easy for children
Distance ▪ 2-mile loop
Hiking time ▪ I hour
Elevation gain ▪ I20 feet
Hikable ▪ Year-round
Map ▪ Santa Clara County Park

At 9000 acres, Joseph D. Grant Park is the largest Santa Clara County park, and it sits in the Diablo Range with high, wooded ridges and sheltered valleys. The park headquarters is in an old ranch house, which also contains a museum of the region's wildlife. There are more than 40 miles of trails in the park, and they range from short walks around the headquarters to long, strenuous hikes to the high ridges. The trails are for the most part old

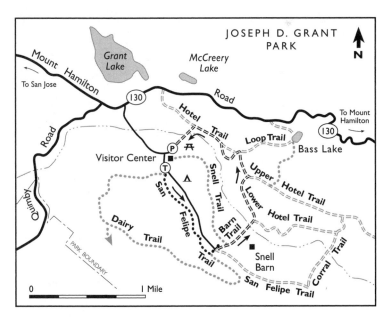

ranch roads, and are broad and well kept. Most follow gentle grades, and equestrians and bicyclists use some extensively.

Take the Alum Rock Avenue exit off I-680 and go east about 2 miles to Mount Hamilton Road. Turn right on Mount Hamilton Road and go 8 miles to the park entrance. Park by the visitor center.

Head out from the parking lot west toward the old barn and corral. Turn south (left) at the old corrals to the trailhead for the San Felipe Trail. This trail follows the road to the family camping area at about 0.25 mile. The campground is located to the left of the trail in a grove of trees.

Follow the trail through oak and grassland.

As you pass the campground the trail enters a small, grassy depression that has several oaks scattered over it. This meadow is an emerald island during the spring and is carpeted with splotches of blue, yellow, orange, and white flowers.

Continue on the San Felipe Trail to the Barn Trail, which takes off to the left at just past 0.75 mile. The Barn Trail passes by the large, white Snell Barn that was built in the 1800s, and still is in use by the park for hay storage.

The Barn Trail gently drops down to the valley toward the Hotel Trail. San Felipe Creek crosses the trail at about 1 mile. This crossing can be muddy during wet weather, but at other times children may want to explore along the wet edges of the creek to hunt for frogs and other small water creatures. At about 1.25 mile the Barn Trail dead-ends at the Lower Hotel Trail. Turn left here, and follow along the edge of the valley until you reach the Upper Hotel Trail at about 1.5 miles.

Turn left on the Upper Hotel Trail and return to the parking area.

41 NORTH RIM TRAIL TO EAGLE ROCK

Type ▪	Day hike
Difficulty ▪	Moderate for children
Distance ▪	2.25-mile loop
Hiking time ▪	2 hours
Elevation gain ▪	340 feet
Hikable ▪	Year-round
Map ▪	Santa Clara County Park

The land for Alum Rock Park was first acquired in 1872, and the canyon of Penitencia Creek has been a popular outing for families since then. The name for the park, which was known for years simply as "The Reservation," comes from a huge 625-foot-high rock that stands on the north side of the canyon where the park's entrance roads join. Alum Rock and the taller Eagle Rock nearby are both of volcanic origin and have withstood erosion as surrounding sedimentary material has been washed away. After World War II, visitors with their cars overran the park, and fragile

Picnic sites are a great place to end your hikes.

plant communities were almost destroyed as steep hillsides and unstable soils eroded from overuse. Since then parking has been limited to control the number of visitors, and Penitencia Creek remains a charming creek that flows over large boulders through a shady canyon. More than 18 miles of trails wind through the 700 acres of the park, and one, Creek Trail, is designated as a National Recreation Trail.

Take Berryessa Road exit off I-680 to Capitol Avenue. Turn left on Capitol Avenue and drive south to Penitencia Creek Road. Turn left on Penitencia Creek Road and continue past Penitencia Creek County Park to Alum Rock Park. Stay on Penitencia Creek Road as it winds through Alum Rock Park until it ends at Alum Rock Avenue. Take a left on Alum Rock Road and continue to the parking lot at the end of the road.

The North Rim Trail leads out of the upstream end of the parking lot as it heads uphill. After about 100 yards a service road that is closed to hikers leads off to the right, and the North Rim Trail to the left. Stay to the left as the trail continues a gentle climb above the canyon below.

At about 0.5 mile you reach a level area with several large buckeye trees that provide shade for a short rest. Have the children look for buckeye seeds. These are the largest seeds produced by any tree in North America. The whole pod is one seed.

At the flat area the Weather Loop Trail leads off to the right uphill. Take this short loop as it reaches a high ledge near the park boundary at about 0.75 mile. The views are excellent from here as the ledge overlooks the Santa Clara Valley. Have the children pick out familiar landmarks.

Continue on the Loop Trail until it rejoins the North Rim Trail at about 1 mile. There are several picnic tables at the junction where you can take a refreshment break. Have the children guess how the old palm trees on the hillside above came to be there. (There was an old ranch site and house there.)

Continue on the North Rim Trail to a fork at about 1.25 miles. Take the right fork on the Eagle Rock Trail to a steep climb to Eagle Rock, where—on a clear day—you can see across the Santa Clara Valley to the Santa Cruz Mountains to the west.

Return to the fork in the trail and take a sharp right turn as the North Rim Trail heads downhill below Eagle Rock. The upthrust of rock on the downhill side of the trail here is volcanic in origin, and hikers should stay off the crumbly material.

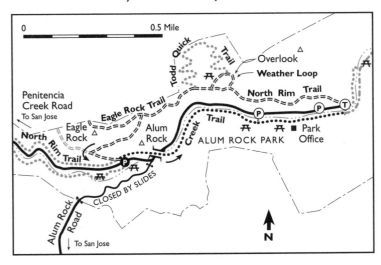

At the junction near 1.5 miles, take a left and then another left after about 200 yards. You are now on the Creek Trail, which will take you upstream as it passes just below Alum Rock, and then crosses the park road at about 1.75 miles. The old bridge here was built in the 1880s for the Alum Rock Steam Railroad. The railroad once went through a tunnel on the south side of the bridge, and a plaque on the crumbled rock tells the story of the old railroad.

The Creek Trail takes you back to the parking lot, as it winds along the creek banks that are shaded by tall sycamore trees and colored by wildflowers in the spring and early summer. As you walk along the trail you can talk to your children about what a train trip along the creek in the late 1800s may have been like.

ALAMEDA COUNTY

42 CANYON VIEW TRAIL TO LITTLE YOSEMITE

Type ▪ Day hike
Difficulty ▪ Moderate for children
Distance ▪ 3-mile loop
Hiking time ▪ 2 hours
Elevation gain ▪ 400 feet
Hikable ▪ Year-round
Map ▪ East Bay Regional Park District

Alameda Creek, the largest stream in the county, winds through the southern part of 5024-acre Sunol Regional Wilderness, home to a large array of wildlife, even an occasional mountain lion and bobcat. The creek offers excellent birding, with thirty to forty species, including the brightly colored yellow-billed magpie, seen along it often in a single morning. Great boulders of serpentine and schist indicate a turbulent geological past, as do the massive basalt outcroppings at Indian Joe Cave Rocks. There are also sandstone outcroppings with marine fossils that indicate the region was once under water. This hike takes you into the region known as "Little Yosemite," a narrow gorge on Alameda Creek with huge boulders and rushing water.

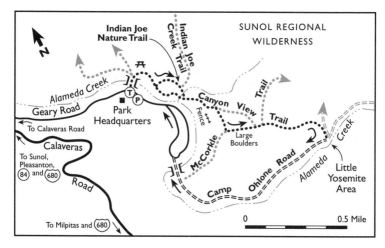

Take the Calaveras Road exit south off I-680, and after about 5 miles turn left on Geary Road. Follow Geary Road to the end and enter the park. Park near the park headquarters, before the end of the road.

From the rest rooms and parking area near the park headquarters, cross Alameda Creek on the large metal footbridge and turn right on the Canyon View Trail. This trail leads along the north bank of the creek, and after about 200 yards you can go down to the creek from the trail. The children will like to explore here, but tell them there will be other places to play along the creek farther along on the trail.

The Indian Joe Nature Trail leads off to the left on the opposite side of the trail. You may take this side trip and return to the Canyon View Trail at about 0.25 mile, or you may continue along the bank of the creek until the trail begins to head uphill at 0.25 mile.

The climb here is moderately taxing as the trail leads up the side of a steep ravine. At about 0.5 mile the trail forks. Take the right, and continue up the steep section of the trail. Several hundred yards past the fork, the trail levels out and veers to the left. To your right you can see a lightly used trail that leads along a fence to some huge boulders in the midst of a small grove of oak trees. Take the lightly used trail to the right.

The moss-covered boulders are a favorite climbing spot for children, as are those about 220 yards farther uphill. The McCorkle Trail crosses the meadow here as it heads uphill to join the Canyon View Trail at just under 0.75 mile. Take it to the junction, and then take a right on the Canyon View Trail as it leads around the contour of a steep slope. An occasional oak shades this section of the

It's a bird's world.

trail, and the hillsides are covered with bright wildflowers in the spring and early summer.

At about 1.25 miles the trail crosses a saddle and begins a slow descent down the other side of the ridge. From here you can see the canyon that has been cut by Alameda Creek. Just before 1.5 miles you reach a trail junction. Take a sharp right here as a spur of the Canyon View Trail leads down to Alameda Creek and the Little Yosemite area. You reach the creek and the large granite boulders that give the area its name just past 1.5 miles. This is a good rest stop and lunch break, for the children will like to explore along the banks of the creek and climb on the large boulders.

After heavy winter rains the creek roars over the large boulders and the children should not attempt to climb out onto them. The water level falls fairly quickly after the rains subside, and the children can explore the creek and boulders safely.

From the Little Yosemite area take a right on the Camp Ohlone Road as it follows Alameda Creek back toward the park headquarters. The East Bay Water District requests that you not wade or swim in the creek because it is part of the city water supply.

At about 2.75 miles the road crosses Alameda Creek on a large bridge with a hikers' stile. From here you can follow the paved road to your right, or you can hike along Alameda Creek back to the parking area.

43 BOARDWALK/MUSKRAT TRAILS LOOP

Type ■ Day hike
Difficulty ■ Easy for children
Distance ■ 1.5-mile loop
Hiking time ■ 1 hour
Elevation gain ■ Level
Hikable ■ Year-round
Map ■ East Bay Regional Park District

Coyote Hills Regional Park is a 966-acre wildlife sanctuary that includes grass-covered hills, freshwater marshes, fallow fields, and willow runs. Each of these provides habitat for a variety of

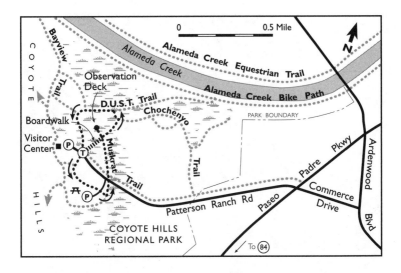

birds and mammals throughout the year. It is during the winter and migration times, though, that thousands of birds can be seen in the park as they come to feed and rest. Trails and a boardwalk lead visitors through all the major habitat areas in the park and up into the rocky miniature mountain range known as the Coyote Hills. When de Anza's exploration party first looked out from the East Bay hills, they saw the surrounding marshes as they were flooded at high tide, and mistakenly thought the hills were islands that stood up from the southern end of the bay.

Take the Paseo Padre Parkway exit off CA 84 (Nimitz Freeway) and go north 1.5 miles to Patterson Ranch Road. Turn west on Patterson Ranch Road and continue 1 mile to the visitor center.

Cross the road from the visitor center to the beginning of the boardwalk. This walk takes you over a freshwater marsh that is full of life. The boardwalk follows a winding course as it crosses small ponds, through reeds and cattails that are above the heads of the children, and over large open bodies of water. Have the children look for large flying insects such as dragonflies and for various water birds that feed in the nourishing marshes.

Several benches are located along the 0.25-mile boardwalk, and these make excellent observation points for bird watchers.

The boardwalk ends at the Muskrat Trail. You can take a short side trip by turning left and heading along the trail into the marsh for about 200 yards. From the observation deck there you can

Watch for the many varieties of grasses that grow in the region.

watch the wide variety of waterfowl and shorebirds that feed in the marsh. This is especially exciting during the fall migration and the spring breeding periods.

Return to the junction of the boardwalk and Muskrat Trail and head straight on Muskrat Trail as it leads you across the higher and drier portions of the marsh. During the rainy season this trail can be flooded as the marsh becomes a large, shallow lake, so check with the visitor center to make sure you can cross it without getting your feet soaked.

New growth springs forth along the trail after the winter lake has dried up, and many birds come to feed on the plants and small insects that become active then. If you don't have binoculars of your own for watching the birds, you can rent them at the visitor center.

Have the children observe the vast quantities of cattails and reeds, and discuss with them how the Native Americans used this almost inexhaustible supply of material for food and shelter.

At about 1.25 miles the Muskrat Trail crosses the road, passes a trail that leads off to the right, and then turns sharply to the right as it heads back toward the visitor center.

44 TIDELANDS TRAIL

Type ▪	Day hike
Difficulty ▪	Easy for children
Distance ▪	1.25-mile loop
Hiking time ▪	1 hour
Elevation gain ▪	150 feet
Hikable ▪	Year-round
Map ▪	San Francisco Bay National Wildlife Refuge

The Don Edwards–San Francisco Bay National Wildlife Refuge contains more than 23,000 acres of marshes, mud flats, salt ponds, sloughs, and open water. It is the largest urban refuge in the National Wildlife Refuge system, and hundreds of thousands of birds that travel along the Pacific Flyway visit the refuge each year to rest and feed. Many others live there year-round, including the rare bay clapper rail. The American avocet is common here, and has been chosen as the refuge's emblem. Stilts, egrets, herons, terns, and many kinds of ducks are found in huge numbers in the refuge. Hikers and birders should always stay on the marked trails, especially

Walkways lead through a world of water and grass.

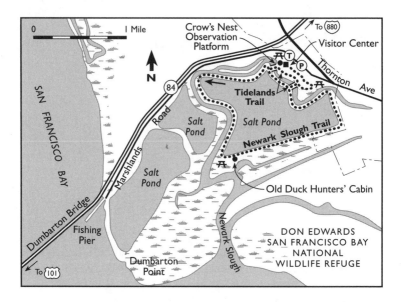

during the nesting season. Nesting birds complain vociferously when people get near their nests, and some have been known to dive-bomb intruders.

From CA 84 go south on Thornton Avenue just before the Dumbarton Bridge and follow the signs on Marshlands Road to the visitor center.

From the parking area take the path to the visitor center, where there is plenty of information about the refuge and the bay, and start your hike from the overlook behind the center. Go left and head uphill to the high point of the refuge. From the crow's nest observation platform here, you can look out over Newark Slough and the salt ponds that make up most of the refuge.

There are picnic tables here, so you can have a snack before you head out around the ponds, or you can stop here at the end of your hike.

As the trail leads downhill, it passes by several information panels that explain the history of the region and by an outcropping of chert, a material that was used for arrowheads by Native Americans.

Take the Tidelands Trail as it drops to marsh level and crosses a bridge to the levee. Stay to the right as the trail leads along the levee, with a marsh and tidal slough on your right and a salt-evaporator pond on your left.

These ponds were once used by Leslie Salt Company to produce thousands of tons of salt by collecting salt water during the warm summer months and letting the water evaporate, leaving large amounts of salt. Now they are the home to many species of birds that feed on the brine flies and brine shrimp that live in the shallow, salty water.

The trail continues around the edge of the salt pond, and at about 0.75 mile comes to an old duck hunters' cabin at the edge of the slough. The cabin has been left much as it was at the turn of the century, and the story of duck hunting in the area is told on information panels here.

Just past the cabin an old salt company pump house has been converted into a picnic shelter where you can have lunch as you watch the birds in the marsh.

Continue on around the salt pond until you come to another bridge across Newark Slough. Take a right, cross the bridge, and then take either a right or left to return to the visitor center and the picnic tables there.

45 HIGH RIDGE/MEYERS RANCH/ DRY CREEK TRAILS LOOP

Type ▪	Day hike
Difficulty ▪	Difficult for children
Distance ▪	2.25-mile loop
Hiking time ▪	2 hours
Elevation gain ▪	500 feet
Hikable ▪	Year-round
Map ▪	East Bay Regional Park District

Dry Creek Pioneer Regional Park is the eastern portion of this dual park and offers several attractions not found in Garin Regional Park to the west. Jordon Pond is a short hike from the visitor center, and offers fishing opportunities to all comers. This pond sits in the midst of a landscaped area with picnic tables. Largemouth bass, bluegill, and sunfish have become a naturally reproducing population in the pond, and channel catfish are planted in the pond once or twice a year. Another feature of the Dry Creek section of the park is the Chabot Fault, an offshoot of

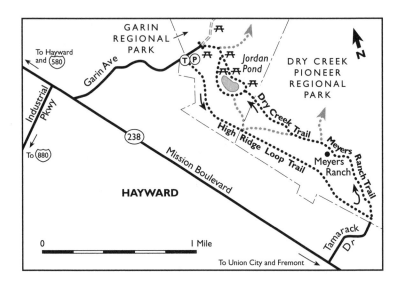

the Hayward Fault, which runs beneath the High Ridge Loop Trail near the crest of the ridge.

Take the CA 238 exit off I-580. Continue on CA 238, which becomes Mission Boulevard, past the light at Industrial Parkway. Garin Avenue is the next street on the left. Turn left and go 1 mile to the park entrance.

From the parking area, head back toward the park entrance on the entrance road for about 100 yards to the beginning of the High Ridge Loop Trail. Take a left, go through a cattle gate, and head across an open meadow. This area is full of wildflower blooms during the spring and early summer.

At just under 0.5 mile the trail reaches the crest of a low ridge and crosses the Chabot Fault, a branch of the Hayward Fault. The Hayward Fault is located about 1 mile to the west of the park and has been the cause of several major quakes in the past century. The seismic activity in the area makes the unstable, steep slopes of the park less than desirable land for building.

Just past the crest the High Ridge Loop Trail ends at the Meyers Ranch Trail. Take a left onto Meyers Ranch Trail as it follows along the ridge crest.

At just past 1.5 miles the Meyers Ranch Trail veers to the right, and the Dry Creek Trail heads straight. Continue straight on Dry Creek Trail and head back toward the old Meyers Ranch.

If you wish to take a longer hike you can continue on the High

Ridge Trail to about 1.75 miles and take the trail to Gossip Rock, where Native Americans met to grind acorns on the sandstone rocks under old bay trees.

If you take the shorter route, the trail leads down the side of the ridge and follows along Dry Creek. It crosses the creek several times on bridges before it reaches the old ranch house (now a park residence). Continue past the house and corral several hundred feet to the Dry Creek Trail, which leads off to the left. The trail leads beside the creek beneath the shade of oak and sycamore trees until it reaches Jordon Pond at about 2 miles.

Jordon Pond is a landscaped area with lawns and picnic tables and is a good place to eat lunch. Children like to explore around the edges of the ponds and watch the waterfowl there as you rest.

After a break at the pond it is just a short walk back to the parking area.

Are there really newts at Newt Pond?

46 MARSH TRAIL LOOP

Type ■ Day hike
Difficulty ■ Moderate for children
Distance ■ 4-mile loop; side trip to interpretive center, 1 mile
Hiking time ■ 2 hours
Elevation gain ■ Level
Hikable ■ Year-round
Map ■ East Bay Regional Park District

The 817 acres of Hayward Regional Shoreline was a huge, thriving marshland before the American Salt Company was established in 1865. This company built dikes on the outer edges of the saltwater marshes that were filled with cordgrass to trap salt water. The dikes formed large ponds of stagnant water that was pumped through a series of evaporation ponds. Salt was then harvested from the ponds. The American Salt Company used the site until 1927, when Leslie Salt Company leased the ponds. Because Leslie already operated a large number of ponds in the area, the site was never actively used again. By the 1970s several governmental

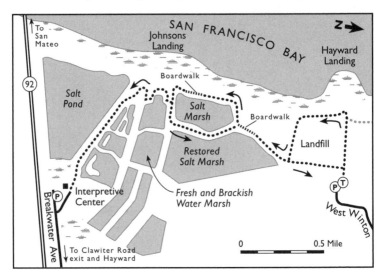

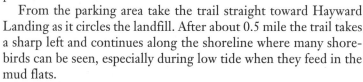

Visitor centers are a good place to begin your hike.

agencies banded together to purchase the site. They developed a management plan that involved rebuilding the site to its original marshland status. Today the Hayward Regional Shoreline includes the largest restored salt marsh on the West Coast.

Take the West Winton Avenue exit off I-880 and go west to the park entrance.

From the parking area take the trail straight toward Hayward Landing as it circles the landfill. After about 0.5 mile the trail takes a sharp left and continues along the shoreline where many shorebirds can be seen, especially during low tide when they feed in the mud flats.

At about 0.75 mile the trail takes another sharp left and then intersects with another trail at a "T" near 1 mile. Take a right at the "T" and head out across the largest restored salt marsh on the West Coast. At just under 1.25 miles you cross a boardwalk, and the trail forks. Take a right to head toward the bay. The trail bends to the left after about 200 yards and heads toward another boardwalk at about 1.5 miles. This area of the marsh is full of activity as birds flock there to feed on the many small sea animals that live in the life-giving mud of the marsh.

Have the children bend down on the boardwalks to see how many different forms of life they can identify. These may be plants or animals, and some may be very small.

The trail turns to the left about 100 yards past the second board-walk, and then another trail leads off to the right almost immediately. This trail leads to the interpretive center, where you can learn about life in the marsh and the history of the area.

If you do not wish to take the 1-mile round trip to the interpretive center, continue straight for another 200 yards until the trail turns left and heads back across the restored salt marsh. If you head for the interpretive center, the trail will lead past the edge of a freshwater and brackish marsh. Have the children see if they can tell the difference in the plants that live here as opposed to those that live in the saltwater marsh.

After you view exhibits at the interpretive center, return by the same route until you reach the trail junction at the saltwater marsh. Take a right at the junction to return by a different route that takes you through the center of the marsh.

Have the children look for plants and animals that were described in the exhibits as you make the return trip.

47 EAST SHORE TRAIL

Type ▪	Day hike
Difficulty ▪	Moderate for children
Distance ▪	3 miles, round trip
Hiking time ▪	3 hours
Elevation gain ▪	Minimal
Hikable ▪	Year-round
Map ▪	East Bay Regional Park District

This 315-acre lake has an intimate feel, with many nooks and crannies along its shoreline that form bays and inlets, and an island in the middle. The lake was formed in 1874, when Anthony Chabot, a hydraulic engineer who had worked in the gold country, aimed gigantic water hoses on the hills above San Leandro Creek and washed thousands of tons of debris into the creek bed. He then imported a huge herd of wild horses, which he ran back and forth across the loose debris to pack it into an earthen dam. The lake behind the dam, and the revegetating hills above, were off limits to the public from the time the lake was built until the

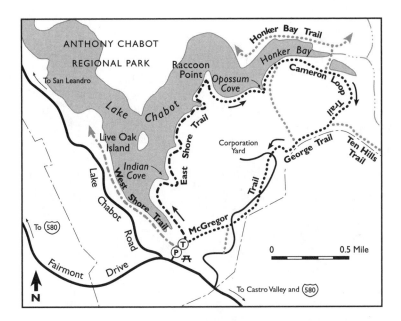

mid-1960s, when legislation was passed that opened the area to the public for controlled recreational uses. Today Anthony Chabot Regional Park is one of the most popular fishing spots in the East Bay, and boats and canoes can be rented for trips into the various narrow inlets and bays. Hiking is also a favorite activity here, and most of the trails around the lake are paved, making them accessible to wheelchairs and strollers.

Take the Fairmont Drive exit off I-580 and head east. Fairmont Drive becomes Lake Chabot Road. Continue on Lake Chabot Road to the park entrance.

The East Shore Trail leads from the parking area along the shore of Lake Chabot toward Honker Bay. It leads close to the shores of several small inlets and coves, and past fishing piers that jut out into the lake as it follows the contours of the hill above the shoreline.

At about 0.25 mile you pass Indian Cove, and you get a good view of Live Oak Island offshore. Have the children explore along the shallow waters in the coves and inlets and look for birds in the chaparral and oaks uphill from the lake, as well as in the cattails and reeds along the shore.

At about 1 mile the trail turns sharply to the right as it comes to Raccoon Point. You may want to walk out to the point and take a rest stop here before continuing on around Honker Bay. You can

When the water is low you can explore the shoreline as you circle the lake.

watch the boat traffic on the lake and see if you can identify any of the hawks that are soaring above.

Return to the trail and go to your left to continue the hike. If any of the children are tired, this is a good spot to turn around and head back to the car.

The trail heads through groves of oak that furnish good shade, and a creek comes into the lake at Opossum Cove at 1.25 miles. Another trail leads off to the right just past the cove, but continue along the shore until you come to the bridge across the headwaters of Honker Bay just past 1.5 miles.

As you head across the footbridge you enter into open grassland that is exposed to the southern sun. Here the temperature is appreciably warmer, and it is a good spot to take a break in the winter as the children explore along the shallow waters of the creek as it enters Honker Bay. In the summer they may want to play in the water, but park regulations prohibit any swimming or wading.

To return you may retrace your route along the shoreline, or you may take an alternate route that leads into the hills above the shore. For the alternate route, take a left turn onto the Cameron Loop Trail as you return across the bridge. Follow this trail around the contour of the hill above the flat valley drained by the creek to just over 2 miles. There the trail joins with the Ten Hills Trail to the left and the George Trail to the right. Turn right onto the George Trail.

At 2.25 miles a trail leads off to the right back to the lake, but continue straight as the trail climbs a gentle grade before making a sharp turn at 2.5 miles. After the turn the trail rounds a hill and comes to a paved road that leads to the county corporation yard. Cross the road and stay on the trail (now McGregor Trail) as it follows along the road and crosses it several times, before a trail leads off to the right at 2.75 miles.

Take this trail back to the parking area.

48 CRAB COVE TO ROEMER BIRD SANCTUARY TRAIL

Type ▪	Day hike
Difficulty ▪	Moderate for children
Distance ▪	4 miles, round trip
Hiking time ▪	3 hours
Elevation gain ▪	Level
Hikable ▪	Year-round
Map ▪	East Bay Regional Park District

This area of the San Francisco Bay shoreline has a long history of recreational use. From the 1870s to the 1930s it featured fancy swimming pools, restaurants, hotels, and Neptune Beach, a large amusement center with a stadium, skating rink, merry-go-round, and other rides. It was often referred to as the Coney Island of the West. During World War II the military turned the area into a maritime training center, and the building that is now used as the Crab Cove visitor center and for naturalists' programs was a military hospital. In 1959 the beach became a state park, and in 1967 the East Bay Regional Park District assumed control. Crown Memorial State Beach is now a popular park, and people come to it for many activities, especially in warm weather. The marshes, freshwater lagoons, marine sanctuary at Crab Cove, and bird sanctuary at the beach are popular for hiking. While the area is crowded at midday and on warm summer days, hikers find solitude here in the early mornings or early evenings; on cloudy, overcast days; and at almost any time in the winter.

Take Webster Street through the Posey Tunnel to Alameda.

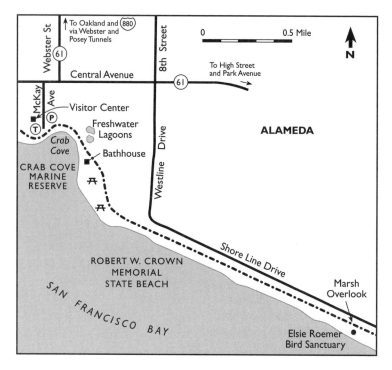

 Continue on Webster to Central Avenue and turn right. Go one block on Central and turn left on McKay Avenue. Continue on McKay to the park entrance.

From the parking lot head toward Crab Cove and turn left on the paved trail as it leads through a developed area with many picnic tables and a bathhouse. Two small freshwater lagoons are on the left just before the bathhouse, and you may want to return to explore them at the end of the hike.

Crab Cove is a marine reserve, and you may not collect any marine animals or plants from the area.

At about 0.5 mile the trail veers to the left as it follows along the top of the beach and heads toward the marsh overlook at the Roemer Bird Sanctuary.

Follow along the path as you keep an eye out for the many shore-birds and water birds that come to the beach to feed, and at 2 miles the marsh overlook is on your right. Take a right and cross the beach to the overlook.

The marsh and the mud flats of the bay around you are part of the Elsie Roemer Bird Sanctuary. This sanctuary is home to dozens

Look for small objects as you stroll along the beach.

of species of shorebirds and water birds, and the overlook is an excellent spot to bring your binoculars and bird guides and spend an hour or so seeing how many species you can identify.

After your stop at the overlook, return to the trail and retrace your route to the parking area.

On a warm day your children can swim after changing at the bathhouse, or they can simply wade along the edge of the beach.

49 REDWOOD CREEK HEADWATERS TRAIL LOOP

Type ■	Day hike
Difficulty ■	Moderate for children
Distance ■	2.75-mile loop
Hiking time ■	3 hours
Elevation gain ■	700 feet
Hikable ■	Year-round
Map ■	East Bay Regional Park District

In 1855 a hollow tree stump, 33.5 feet in diameter, was discovered near Redwood Peak, and the virgin stand of redwoods in what is now Redwood Regional Park may have been one of the most magnificent in the whole redwood region. Sailors used two of these magnificent trees as markers as they attempted to miss Blossom Rock near Alcatraz Island. The trees would have been 16 miles from the Golden Gate. This stand of redwoods was logged

To Huckleberry Botanic Preserve

To Tilden
Regional Park

Skyline Trail

REDWOOD REGIONAL PARK

Skyline Gate
Staging Area

Girls
Camp

Eucalyptus Trail

Stream Trail

Stream Trail

Redwood Creek

French Trail

Trail

Star Flower Trail

West

Tres Sendas

French Trail

Ridge

Skyline

Trail

Redwood Peak Trail

Redwood △
Peak

Moon Gate
Staging Area

Blvd

0   0.5 Mile

To Joaquin Miller Road

between 1840 and 1860 as at least ten sawmills operated in the
area. Large, raucous shantytowns sprang up around the mills to
house the workers. These were violent times in the East Bay, and
nature had yet to be tamed. Grizzly bears were known to have
prowled by night, occasionally killing cattle, hogs, and horses,
and mountain lions often awakened sleeping loggers. Even California condors were said to have flown overhead in groups of as
many as fifty—more than exist now. The second-growth redwoods that now stand in the park are more than 100 years old, and
offer a cool respite from the busy world of the urban East Bay.

Take the Redwood Road exit off CA 13 (Warren Freeway), and
follow Redwood Road east to Skyline Boulevard. Turn left on Skyline Boulevard and follow it along the crest of the Oakland Hills,
veering to the right at the junction of Skyline Boulevard and
Joaquin Miller Road. Continue about 2.5 miles along Skyline Boulevard to the Skyline Gate Staging Area on the right-hand side of
the road.

From the Skyline Gate Staging Area take the Stream Trail
straight ahead as it heads downhill past the meadow where the
"Girls Camp," a stone hut with rest room and water, is located at
0.5 mile. The trail follows the upper reaches of Redwood Creek
along this section as it passes through an old eucalyptus grove that

has been cleared into a grove of tall redwoods. These provide shade for the moisture-loving ferns and trilliums that grow along the hillsides and creek.

At about 0.75 mile the trail begins a short, steep descent to a small open meadow, and the Eucalyptus Trail leads off to the left. Stay on the Stream Trail, and at 1 mile the Tres Sendas Trail leads off to the right. Take the Tres Sendas Trail as it crosses the north fork of Redwood Creek and heads up the south fork. This is a good spot to take a short break and let the children explore around the banks of the creeks, which are little more than trickles in mid- to late summer, but which flow strongly after winter rains. They can search for different kinds of ferns along the creek banks, and turn over old logs to find salamanders and creepy crawlers.

Return to the Stream Trail and turn right. After about 200 yards take the Star Flower Trail to the left as it heads up a small ravine. At about 1.25 miles turn right on the French Trail as it climbs a steep hillside out of a ravine. Continue past the Redwood Peak Trail as it leads off to the left at just under 1.5 miles, and cross a ravine that has a thick stand of huckleberries, a cousin of the domestic blueberry. The children can taste this small, blue berry if the birds haven't eaten them all, but make sure they are picking them from the small bushes that look like blueberry bushes.

Stop and look inside the log.

The trail comes to a ridge and then drops down into another ravine as it follows a small stream to Redwood Creek's south fork at about 1.75 miles.

Turn right on Tres Sendas Trail at the south fork and go about 100 yards to the junction of the French Trail. Take a left and head up through a thick covering of evergreen broadleaf bay and tanoak. As you reach the ridge just before 2 miles you enter a pine forest.

At 2 miles take a right on the West Ridge Trail to return to the parking area.

50 HUCKLEBERRY PATH NATURE TRAIL

Type ▪	Day hike
Difficulty ▪	Easy for children
Distance ▪	1.75-mile loop
Hiking time ▪	1 hour
Elevation gain ▪	400 feet
Hikable ▪	Year-round
Map ▪	East Bay Regional Park District

Two small knolls stand sentinel over this delightful ecological relic. Because it is located due east of the Golden Gate, Huckleberry Botanic Regional Preserve receives heavy winter rains and cool summer fogs that provide the moisture needed to support a plant community that is unique to the East Bay. Brittleleaf and pallid manzanita (which survives in only two places in the world) thrive on the barren, rocky knolls, where other plants such as huckleberry, silktassel, and chinquapin will eventually replace them. This occurs as the leaf litter deposited by the manzanita composts into richer and moister soil. Many of the plants found in the preserve can only be seen in Northern California, some only in the East Bay, and the variety of rare and beautiful plants in the preserve is remarkable for such a small area. In the early 1970s developers threatened the preserve, but the East Bay Regional Park District obtained the fragile preserve and the narrow footpath that leads to it. Early spring is the most popular time to visit the preserve, and it is often crowded along the trails in February.

Chaparral so dense you can't break through it

Take the Fish Ranch Road exit off CA 24 just east of the Caldecott Tunnel. At 0.8 mile take a left off Fish Ranch Road onto Grizzly Peak Boulevard and go for 2.5 miles to the intersection of Grizzly Peak Boulevard and Skyline Boulevard. Make another left turn and go for about 0.5 mile, past the entrance to Sibley Volcanic Regional Preserve, to the park entrance.

Take the Huckleberry Path Nature Trail from the parking area as it leads through batches of blackberries, coyote brush, and poison hemlock. If you don't know what poison hemlock is, you may want to look it up in a field guide so you can readily identify it for your children.

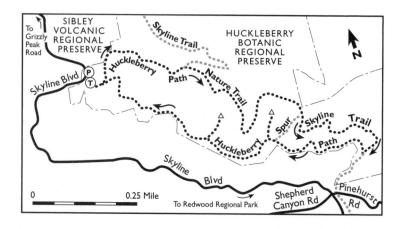

After about 200 yards the trail forks. Take the left fork as it begins a series of switchbacks down the side of a forested canyon toward the Skyline Trail and then climbs out of the Sibley Volcanic Regional Preserve. At just under 0.5 mile the Huckleberry Path Nature Trail joins the Skyline Trail. Stay to the right and begin a gentle climb around the northern contour of the knolls that dominate the preserve. Broad-crowned bay trees provide excellent shade for the many fern that grow on this northern slope, and there are occasional openings through the canopy that provide views of the Contra Costa hills.

The trail passes a spur to the right at about 0.75 mile. Take this spur if the children are getting tired. It connects with the upper section of the Huckleberry Path and cuts a little more than 0.25 mile off the hike. Turn right as the spur dead-ends at the Huckleberry Path. Otherwise continue straight until the Huckleberry Path takes a sharp turn back to the right at about 1 mile as the Skyline Trail continues straight ahead.

Take the Huckleberry Path as it climbs steeply for a short distance before leveling out for its return to the parking area. It is along this upper section of the trail that the most interesting plants in the preserve are found. Have the children find examples of the three different kinds of manzanita that grow along here. You can identify them from the park brochure that is found at the trailhead. Discuss that these plants are found in only a few places and why they should be preserved.

Just before 1.25 miles a spur leads off to the first of the two knolls that rise above the parks. The views from these are excellent, and the rare manzanitas are most abundant here.

Return to the main trail from this 200-yard side trip and turn right to the next spur in about 300 yards.

After making these two side trips, continue back to the parking area.

51 SHORE TRAIL LOOP

Type ▪	Day hike
Difficulty ▪	Easy for children
Distance ▪	0.75-mile loop
Hiking time ▪	I hour
Elevation gain ▪	Minimal
Hikable ▪	Year-round
Map ▪	East Bay Regional Park District

Costanoan Indians who lived along the creek that feeds Lake Temescal used it for bathing and swimming long before the Spanish arrived in the region. The early missionaries named the creek from two Aztec words: tema (to bathe) and call (house). By 1870 Anthony Chabot had dammed the creek to form 13-acre Lake

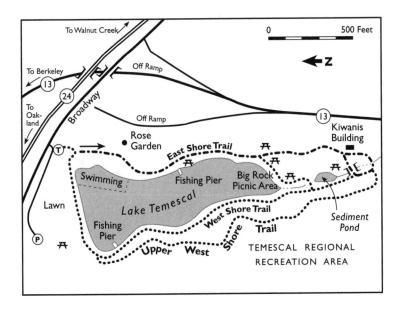

Temescal, which was used as a source of water for the "tiny" town of Oakland. The 48-acre park that surrounds the lake was one of the three original parks of the East Bay Regional Park District and was opened as a recreation area in 1986. Today Temescal Regional Recreation Area is one of the most popular swimming and hiking spots in the East Bay. It was also the only park in the East Bay Regional Park District that was damaged by the October 1991 fire that devastated so much of the Oakland Hills.

Take the Broadway Avenue exit off CA 24 in Oakland. Follow the signs toward CA 13. Park in the lot on the right (north) side of Broadway just before you reach CA 13.

From the parking lot walk to the east shore of the lake to the paved path that leads by the swimming area and rose garden. The Hayward Fault runs beneath the lake just out from the east shore, and the lake sits in a "rift valley" where the fault has long caused sag ponds in depressions. Earth movement is constant, although generally unnoticed, along the fault line, and fault movement evidence is visible along the trail at the south end of the lake.

Follow the trail along the shore of the lake, and at just past 0.25 mile a spur leads off toward the creek at the Big Rock Picnic Area. This spur leads you down to the streamside near the sediment pond. Children love to explore along here in hopes of catching sight of a frog or turtle. After a stop here you can either return to

Many lakes have manicured lawns around them.

the paved trail or walk up the stream around the sediment pond toward the Kiwanis Building and south play area. It is along the paved trail near the building that the fault movement is most evident.

After observing the evidence you can discuss with the children what it means to stand on top of a major earthquake zone, and why the freeway interchange at the northeast end of the park may not have been such a good idea.

Continue around the lake by crossing the footbridge, and there are two trails available. The one to the immediate left follows along the west shore of the lake, and gives the children an opportunity to wade in the shallow waters as they search for water creatures. The one straight ahead climbs the hillside and gives you a view of the whole lake with all its waterfowl.

Take either, or both, of these trails because they are each less than 0.5 mile as they lead back to the parking area.

52 ROUND TOP TRAIL LOOP

Type ▪	Day hike
Difficulty ▪	Moderate for children
Distance ▪	2-mile loop
Hiking time ▪	2 hours
Elevation gain ▪	450 feet
Hikable ▪	Year-round
Map ▪	East Bay Regional Park District

Sibley Volcanic Regional Preserve was one of the first three parks in the East Bay Regional Park District, along with Lakes Temescal and Tilden, and was dedicated in 1936. The 1763-foot-high Round Top Peak dominates this 386-acre preserve. It now stands as a small, rounded hill among the higher peaks of the Oakland Hills, but it once was the most prominent volcano in what is now the East Bay. This volcano erupted beneath a large freshwater lake about 10 million years ago, and geologists have counted eleven separate lava flows and two violent explosions in the long history of Round Top. Because of this extensive, violent history, Round Top has long been a favorite hike for geologists, amateur and professional, as the quarries operated by the Kaiser

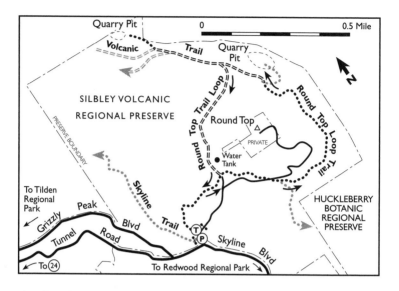

Sand and Gravel Company for years exposed volcanic vents and other features.

Take the Fish Ranch Road exit off CA 24 just east of the Caldecott Tunnel. At 0.8 mile take a left off Fish Ranch Road onto Grizzly Peak Boulevard and go for 2.5 miles to the intersection of Grizzly Peak Boulevard and Skyline Boulevard. Make another left turn, and go to the entrance of the preserve.

Before you begin the hike, pick up the self-guided trail brochure at the visitor center, so that you don't miss any of the geological features of the preserve. From the visitor center take the trail to the right as it follows the paved road toward the large water tank. At just over 0.25 mile the trail crosses the Round Top Trail Loop and the paved road that leads to the water tank.

The first stop on the self-guided tour is at the tank, so take the short side trip to the left up the paved road and then return to the trail. Take a left and continue on the trail as it parallels the road, and then crosses it just past 0.5 mile.

The trail now leads around the lower slopes of Round Top through a mixed forest of bay, toyon, Monterey pine, and eucalyptus that is interrupted by occasional open meadows, which are brilliant palettes of wildflowers in the spring.

Just past 0.75 mile the view opens up and you can see Mount Diablo to the east, and a large, old quarry pit that exposed the interior of Round Top, an old volcano, as it was dug.

Keep trudging to the top where the views are great.

As you pass the old quarry pit, the trail leads through an area of exposed volcanic material and passes the junction of the Volcanic and Round Top Trails at about 1 mile. Go straight ahead on the Volcanic Trail until a spur leads off to the right toward the second quarry pit at about 1.25 miles.

The sides of this quarry show large exposed lava flows and an accumulation of red-baked cinders that indicate there was once a volcanic vent there.

Return to the trail junction and take a right on the Round Top Trail Loop to head back to the parking area.

53 PACK RAT TRAIL LOOP

Type ■	Day hike
Difficulty ■	Easy for children
Distance ■	1-mile loop
Hiking time ■	1 hour
Elevation gain ■	100 feet
Hikable ■	Year-round
Map ■	East Bay Regional Park District

Little Farm, Jewel Lake, and a free-form environmental education center with displays on various aspects of the East Bay's natural history are all found at the nature study area of Tilden Regional Park. Ohlone Indians lived where the study area is now located, but their population declined rapidly after the invasion of the Spanish. After Europeans settled in the East Bay, much of the area

Take a boardwalk through a swamp to view many small water animals.

now covered by Tilden Regional Park was used for grazing, particularly the slopes of Wildcat Canyon. In the 1930s a Civilian Conservation Corps (CCC) camp was built in the canyon, and the CCC planted many trees in the grasslands to protect the watershed. After World War II the Oakland Public Schools and other organizations used the area as a nature school camp. The park district established a full-time nature study program in the area in the early 1960s. There are 740 acres in the nature study area, with 10 miles of trails, a lake, and several ponds and creeks.

Take Wildcat Canyon Road off Grizzly Peak Boulevard. Immediately turn left on Canon Drive and follow it to the parking lot for Little Farm.

This short hike begins at Little Farm and the education center. At Little Farm the children will like to play for a while with the collection of animals that changes with the seasons. Sometimes there are donkeys and pigs; at other times, goats, sheep, and calves. After this playtime, head for the education center, where the children can browse through the displays and learn about the trails.

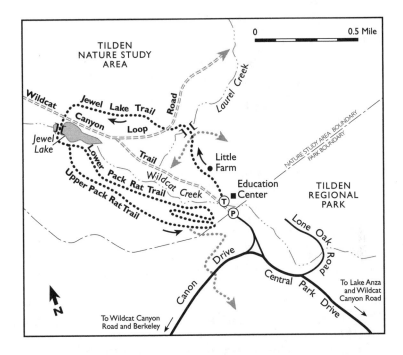

From the center take the Jewel Lake Trail as it leads up a gentle climb and then crosses Laurel Creek at about 0.25 mile and passes Loop Road in another 100 yards. Between Loop Road and Jewel Lake the trail follows in an almost straight line through a shaded forest.

At about 0.5 mile the trail dead-ends into the Upper Pack Rat Trail just above Jewel Lake. Take a left on Upper Pack Rat Trail and cross Loop Road after about 100 feet. As you cross the road the trail becomes an elevated boardwalk that crosses a frog-filled marsh that is a fascinating wilderness for young and old alike.

Take a lunch break at the lake and let the children explore around the edges of the marsh as they look for frogs, turtles, small birds, and flying insects.

After the break you can choose between Upper Pack Rat Trail and Lower Pack Rat Trail for your return to the parking area. Lower Pack Rat Trail follows along Wildcat Creek and offers plenty of opportunity to explore the creek banks, but it is often impassable during wet weather.

If Lower Pack Rat Trail is impassable, take the Upper Pack Rat Trail as it leads along the hillside above the creek and through a forest canopy of evergreen broadleaf trees such as bay and tanoak.

54 SEAVIEW/BIG SPRINGS TRAILS LOOP

Type ▪	Day hike
Difficulty ▪	Moderate for children
Distance ▪	3-mile loop
Hiking time ▪	2 hours
Elevation gain ▪	500 feet
Hikable ▪	Year-round
Map ▪	East Bay Regional Park District

Tilden Regional Park adjoins Wildcat Canyon Regional Park, but the two could hardly be more dissimilar in development. There are miles of paved roads within Tilden, and several highly developed areas with a golf course, artificial Lake Anza, manicured lawns, a botanic garden, and thousands of people. It is hard to get away from the presence of humans here, but most—luckily for those who seek solitude—stay on the canyon floor. Miles of hiking trails crisscross the hills above the developed areas, however, and there hikers can follow almost impenetrable willow growth along creeks, hike under a thick canopy formed by the oak and bay forests on the slopes above the creeks, and stroll through forests

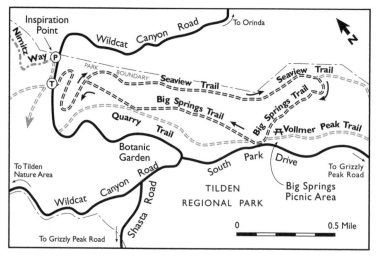

The green grasses of spring turn to golden brown in summer.

formed by exotic trees such as Monterey pine and eucalyptus. All of these are home to a wide variety of wildlife, particularly birds. Wide meadows of open grassland are interspersed with the forests and offer brilliant spring wildflower displays.

Take Wildcat Canyon Road through Tilden Regional Park 1 mile past the botanic garden, to Inspiration Point. Park in the lot at Inspiration Point and walk back 0.25 mile to the gate marked "Dog Run."

The fire road climbs several switchbacks as it heads through a eucalyptus grove toward the ridge. At about 0.25 mile the trail forks; take the Seaview Trail on the left. It leaves the eucalyptus, then goes through several small groves of pine. While walking along this stretch you may have the children explore beneath the eucalyptus trees to see how much fallen debris collects there, and then look at the duff of pine needles beneath the pine trees. Both are fire hazards during the hot summer months, but it is easy to see that much more material gathers beneath the eucalyptus trees.

Both the pine and the eucalyptus are exotic species that are not native to the Berkeley Hills. When the first Europeans came to the San Francisco Bay region, the hills were primarily open grasslands with stands of oak and bay, with willows along the creeks. This was also an artificial state, for the Native Americans periodically burned the hills to rid them of the native chaparral to make it easier to hunt deer and to promote the growth of the oaks, which provided them with acorns.

By 0.5 mile the trail reaches the high point of the ridge, from which there are panoramic views of the San Francisco Bay and the Contra Costa hills.

For the next mile you walk along a relatively level section of trail with open views to both sides. As you hike along, have the children pick out familiar landmarks, including their own neighborhood if it is visible from the ridge.

At about 1.75 miles the Big Springs Trail leads off to the right and makes a sharp turn as it begins to head back toward Inspiration Point. The trail drops down into a canyon as it heads toward the Big Springs Picnic Area at 2.25 miles.

This is a good stopping point for lunch where the children can explore around the forest floor for small insects and crawling animals that can be found in dead and decaying limbs and logs.

After the break, stay to the right on the Big Springs Trail as the Quarry Trail leads off to the left. The trail begins to climb back to the level of the Seaview Trail through a mixed forest of oak, bay, pine, and eucalyptus.

At just past 2.75 miles the Big Springs Trail dead-ends into the Seaview Trail. Take a left to head back to the parking lot.

55 BAY VIEW/MARSH/POINT TRAILS LOOP

Type ■	Day hike
Difficulty ■	Moderate for children
Distance ■	3-mile loop
Hiking time ■	2 hours
Elevation gain ■	Level
Hikable ■	Year-round
Map ■	East Bay Regional Park District

Salt marshes, grasslands, and eucalyptus woodlands are all found in 2147-acre Point Pinole Regional Shoreline Park. While fishing off the concrete pier that extends almost 0.25 mile into the bay is one of the favorite activities of park visitors, bird watching and

Some people prefer to fish as others hike above them.

hiking are close seconds. The square mile of the shoreline is on the Pacific Flyway, and thousands of migrating waterfowl and shorebirds can often be seen there. The wide variety of habitats offers homes to the salt-marsh song sparrow and salt-marsh harvest mouse, native California bunchgrasses such as *Stipa pulchra*, spring wildflowers, and woodland birds not normally found so close to the shore.

Take the Hilltop Drive exit off I-80. Go west to San Pablo Avenue and turn north. From San Pablo turn west on Atlas Road, then south on Giant Highway. On Giant Highway go 0.25 mile to the park entrance.

From the parking area, take the trail to the left that leads toward San Pablo Bay. This is the Bay View Trail; it follows the shoreline for 1 mile to the fishing pier at Pinole Point. About every 200 yards there are short spur trails that lead down to the shoreline, and the children love to take these to see what they can find along the water's edge.

Along this stretch of trail you can watch for numerous shorebirds and water birds, especially during the fall migration and spring breeding times. The trail passes through a grove of trees at about 0.5 mile.

At the fishing pier you can fish at what has been called the best deep-water fishing spot on the bay, or you can simply sit and watch the birds while you take a break or eat lunch.

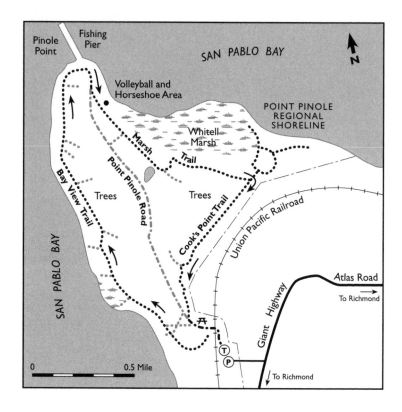

After stopping at the pier, take the Marsh Trail as it leads to the left toward Whitell Marsh. The trail leads past the volleyball and horseshoe areas until it reaches a grove of trees at about 1.5 miles. The Marsh Trail takes off to the left at this fork; the marsh is on the left side of the trail and a grove of trees is on the right.

Continue on the trail as it curves around the edge of the marsh and finally ends near the shore. The children will like to explore along the trail in the marsh to spot small animals in the muck and mud.

Return on the Marsh Trail past the first junction, and take a right at the second. Almost immediately the Marsh Trail leads off to the right and the Cook's Point Trail leads straight ahead. Follow the Cook's Point Trail through the trees and along the railroad track back to the parking area.

CONTRA COSTA/
SOLANO/NAPA
COUNTIES

56 CARQUINEZ OVERLOOK LOOP TRAIL

Type ■	Day hike
Difficulty ■	Easy for children
Distance ■	2.5-mile loop
Hiking time ■	1 hour
Elevation gain ■	Minimal
Hikable ■	Year-round
Map ■	East Bay Regional Park

The Carquinez Strait Regional Shoreline includes bluffs and shorelines between Crockett and Martinez. The hills rise high above the water of Carquinez Strait, which is the gateway to the Sacramento/San Joaquin Delta. The regional shoreline is divided into two separate sections: Bull Valley Staging Area near Crockett, and Carquinez East Staging Area near Martinez; Carquinez Scenic Drive reaches both. There is no through traffic between them, however, because a landslide in 1982 destroyed part of the road and it has not been rebuilt. The trails in both sections of the regional shoreline provide excellent hikes for the fall and winter because they are exposed to the full sun most of the time.

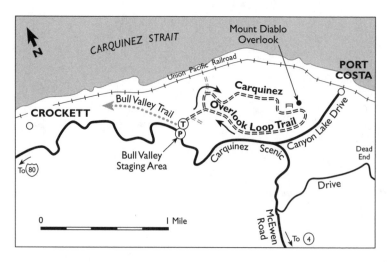

Take I-80 and I-680 to Crockett. From Crockett, take Carquinez Scenic Drive east to the Bull Valley Staging Area. From the parking lot, go through the hikers' gate to the trailhead.

The Bull Valley Trail heads downhill to the left; instead, take the Carquinez Overlook Loop Trail to the right from the trailhead as it begins to follow the contour of the hills above Carquinez Strait.

The trail takes you through open grassland and overlooks Carquinez Strait, the hills on the opposite shore, and Benicia State Recreation Area. The children will like to count the ships and boats that pass by below as you

The bridge over Carquinez Strait

continue along the trail. You may have them keep track of what kinds of vessels they see, which will be everything from small pleasure boats to larger fishing boats to huge oil tankers that are heading to the refineries at Martinez and Antioch.

At 0.1 mile a lightly used trail leads off to the right. Take the main trail to the left.

As the trail leads around the hill, you can look back toward the Carquinez Bridge and see a number of deteriorating, abandoned docks with old fish-processing buildings. Discuss with the children why these were abandoned and talk about how large corporations have taken over the processing of fish that was once done by individual fishermen.

At 0.25 mile the trail crosses a ravine and you can see a large stand of eucalyptus downhill. Coastal scrub chaparral replaces open grassland uphill from the trail along this section.

Just past 0.25 mile a trail leads off to the right. This is the return trail for the loop, so stay to the left as you continue around the hill.

There is plenty of bird life along the trail most of the year, so have the children keep an eye out for large birds, such as hawks and vultures that are often seen soaring above. Among the more interesting small birds that can be seen along the trail is the loggerhead shrike. This small black and gray bird has a beak that is hooked like a hawk's beak; in my youth we called it the "butcher bird." This nickname came from its habit of storing its prey of voles and small mice on thorn trees or barbed wire fences.

Just past 0.5 mile Mount Diablo and the George Miller Bridge, which crosses the upper portion of Carquinez Strait near Antioch, come into view.

A bench overlooks Port Costa and Mount Diablo just past 1 mile, and you can take a short break here to enjoy the view.

The trail turns to the right and heads behind the top of the ridge. Along this section of the trail you overlook Port Costa and several grass-covered ridges that are dotted with thick stands of oak trees. During the winter the trail can be muddy along this section, so you may wish to return to the parking area the way you came rather than completing the loop.

At 2 miles the loop returns to the main trail above the eucalyptus grove. Continue back to the parking lot at about 2.5 miles.

57 BENICIA STATE RECREATION AREA MARSH LOOP TRAIL

Type ▪	Day hike
Difficulty ▪	Easy for children
Distance ▪	1.25-mile loop
Hiking time ▪	1 hour
Elevation gain ▪	Minimal
Hikable ▪	Year-round
Map ▪	Benicia State Recreation Area

The main feature of Benicia State Park is the historic district with the old state capital. A less known part of the park, but still popular with local residents, is the more than 2000-acre wetlands designated as the Benicia State Recreation Area. This area lies just to the west of downtown Benicia and includes a large inlet off the north side of the Carquinez Strait, directly opposite the Carquinez Strait Regional Shoreline. These wetlands are home to many waterfowl and wading birds, as well as a popular stopover and feeding site for migrating waterfowl in the fall. Hikers can walk out into the edge of the marshlands to observe the wildlife.

From I-80 south of Fairfield, take I-780 southeast. In Benicia, take the Columbus Parkway exit off I-780 and follow signs to the recreation area. Park along the road outside the park entrance. Head southeast along the road past the closed vehicle gate and along the paved biking and jogging trail.

At about 0.1 mile a lightly used trail leads to the right off the paved trail. Take this to head down a slight slope, under the low limbs of a large willow, and through a patch of tules and cattails. Plenty of small birds live in this area year-round, but spring nesting season is when they are most obvious. Have the children see how many different birds they can spot. They don't have to know the names of the various birds, but can make up their own classification system (by color, size, where seen, et cetera).

During wet weather this trail is impassable, and you must continue along the paved biking and jogging trail to 0.3 mile where a well-marked trail leads to the right down toward the marsh through open grassland.

If you have taken the first side trail, it joins with the larger trail at just past 0.3 mile. Take a right at this junction and head toward the marsh.

After about another 50 yards there is a small spur trail to the

East Bay parks offer panoramic views of grass-covered hills.

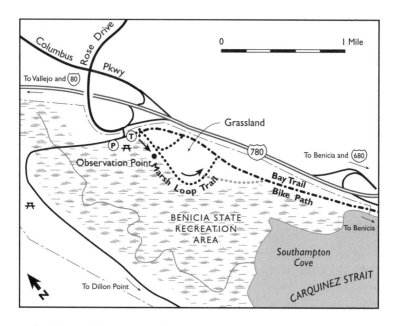

right that leads to an overlook where the children can observe the creek that drains this section of the marsh. Please obey the signs and stay within the marked boundaries. This area is fragile, and hikers are asked not to explore along the edge of the marsh or creek, to avoid further destruction of the habitat.

After spending time at the overlook, return to the Marsh Loop Trail and turn right. At about 0.5 mile there are several medium-sized boulders on both sides of the trail. Have the children explore around both those near the marsh and those on the drier, grassland side to see if they can find any small animals. If they do, have them see if there are any differences in the animals.

Although there is little danger of encountering rattlesnakes here, it is always a good idea to follow safe wilderness practices and watch for them.

Continue along the trail to about 0.7 mile, after the trail has curved to the left to circle an arm of the marsh. At that point a side trail leads to the right across a marshy area with rocks and driftwood that offer a route across the water. If you take this side trek, the trail leads up to grassland on the other side of the marshy area. You can follow this for some distance before it turns to the left and joins with the paved biking and jogging trail. This makes for about a 3-mile loop.

The children can explore around the rocks and driftwood even if you do not cross over the marsh. Have them see how many different small animals they can find and discuss how they may differ from the animals found in the grassland less than 100 feet away.

Return to the main trail and continue to the paved biking and jogging trail at 0.8 mile. Take a left and return to the parking area at 1.25 miles. There are picnic tables past the park entrance kiosk.

58 SUISUN MARSH TRAIL

Type ■	Day hike
Difficulty ■	Moderate for children
Distance ■	2-mile loop
Hiking time ■	2 hours
Elevation gain ■	None
Hikable ■	Year-round
Map ■	Solano County Farmlands and Open Space Foundation

The Solano County Farmlands and Open Space Foundation works with the agricultural community of the region to preserve agricultural land as a productive resource protected from the pressures of development. It also purchases land to help protect and restore marshlands and riparian habitats throughout the county. Rush Ranch is an old ranch that has been purchased by the foundation and opened to the public as an educational and recreational resource. The 2070-acre open space preserve sits along the 84,000-acre Suisun Marsh, the largest single estuarine marsh in the United States with 55,000 acres of wetlands and 29,000 acres of bays and sloughs. In addition to having three developed trails and an education center, Rush Ranch is still a working cattle ranch, with a controlled program oriented around wildlife habitat management.

From I-80 in Fairfield, head southeast on CA 12. Just to the east of Suisun City, take Grizzly Island Road south from CA 12 for 2 miles.

Park near the Rush Ranch visitor center. The Marsh Trail begins behind the visitor center.

This is a marked nature trail, and brochures are generally available

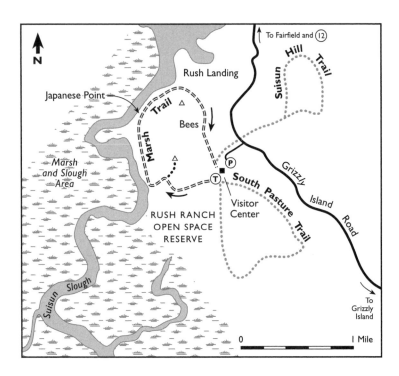

at the visitor center. You may want to call (707-421-1351) before your trip to obtain the self-guiding brochure, however, because they are often out at the center.

The trail heads toward a row of planted eucalyptus through a pasture area, toward a small hill and the marsh.

At 0.25 mile the trail forks and heads around a small knoll. Follow the signs to the left. After about 100 feet a spur trail leads to the top of the knoll, from where you can get a good overview of the marsh. Take this short side trip so the children can see where they are headed, and maybe see some of the many birds that live in the marsh.

Return to the main trail from the knoll and take a right to continue around to the marsh.

The trail immediately enters the marsh area as it curves around the knoll, and the children can begin to look for waterfowl and other water-loving birds as you enter an area of ponds and sloughs. Although you can see many different types of birds here year-round, late fall is a prime time to see thousands and thousands of migrating birds that sometimes cover all open water in the ponds and small sloughs.

Have the children see how many different types of birds they can see on the walk through the marsh area. In the fall this might reach to more than 50, because more than 230 different species of birds have been identified in the area.

They may also see small mammals such as muskrats and river otters along the pond edges if they keep a sharp eye out for them.

At 0.5 mile the trail takes a sharp right turn and heads up the banks of Suisun Slough, a broad, open body of water that is more like a river than a slough. Continue along the slough, all the while watching for different birds.

Just before you reach 1 mile, the trail curves near Japanese Point and heads toward a small knoll at 1.25 miles. There you can climb to the top for another vista of the surrounding marsh and pastureland.

Rush Landing, where boats and barges serving the surrounding ranches landed until well into the twentieth century, is located just around the knoll.

After you round the knoll you head into open pastureland and away from the marsh. Continue to your right, and at about 1.5 miles you cross a dirt dam across a small drainage area. Just beyond

Migration times bring thousands of birds to Suisun Marsh.

the dam there is a digger bee colony. These bees are not aggressive, so you can safely observe them as they enter and leave their nesting areas.

From 1.5 to 2 miles the trail continues across open pasture, and the children can get a close-up look at the living area of some of the region's residents. By getting down on their hands and knees and crawling along the trail, they can look for small tunnels in the matted grass on the side of the trail. Voles and mice make these tunnels as they scurry out onto the open trail to eat fallen seeds. They stay out in the open for only a short time because the hawks that soar overhead are always on the lookout for an easy meal.

The trail returns to the parking lot at 2 miles.

There are two other trails at Rush Ranch that give you a much different perspective of the region. The Suisun Hill Trail takes you into some high hills to the east of the marshlands, where you get an excellent overview of the ranch, and the South Pasture Trail takes you into an area that was partially reclaimed from the marsh.

59 LAKE TRAILS LOOP

Type ■	Day hike
Difficulty ■	Moderate for children
Distance ■	2.5-mile loop
Hiking time ■	2 hours
Elevation gain ■	300 feet
Hikable ■	Year-round
Map ■	Fairfield Department of Parks and Recreation

Rockville Hills Regional Park is a little-known gem of a park that lies in the hills to the west of Fairfield, overlooking the city and the farmlands and marshlands to the east. The 450-mile-long Bay Ridge Trail, which is about two-thirds complete, will run through Rockville Hills Regional Park when it is completed. The park has two lakes (one is more of a small pond) and plenty of oak woodland. During the spring, wildflowers are bountiful on the hillsides, and birds are lively and chatty as they prepare for mating season. Watch overhead for courting raptors such as red-tailed

Picnic tables offer a great rest stop after a steep climb to the top.

hawks and an occasional golden eagle as they perform their mating rituals.

Take the Rockville Hills Road exit off I-80 in Fairfield and head west for 3 miles to Suisun Valley Road. Continue on Rockville Road for about 1 mile past Suisun Valley Road to the park entrance on the left. Find the trailhead at the rear of the parking lot.

The trail begins an immediate steep climb as you head around the contour of a hill. For the first 0.25 mile, you hike through oak woodland and then come into an open area where there are excellent views out over the flat lands to the east.

At about 0.5 mile, after you have made a steep 300-foot climb, the trail levels out and crosses a paved park-maintenance road. Continue straight ahead across the paved road and after about 200 yards come to a small pond on the left. There is a picnic table beneath a large oak tree beside the pond, and children like to explore around the shallow edges in search of frogs and tadpoles, as well as dragonflies and small birds.

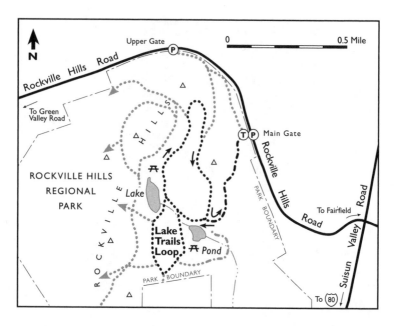

After a short rest, return to the main trail and head right, toward a larger lake, which you reach at 0.75 mile after a short climb.

For a slightly longer hike that gives views to the southwest of the park, you can take the trail that leads off to the left, which winds around a knoll and rejoins the main trail at the upper lake.

Shortly after you reach the lake, the trail forks; stay to the left and continue to the upper end of the lake. There are picnic tables above the lake, and this is an excellent place to stop for a long lunch break while the children explore around the edges of the lake, where the shallow water is home to many small birds and water animals. Although the children should not attempt to swim in the lake, they can wade in the shallows as they search among the reeds and rushes. After a stop at the lake you have the option of returning by the same route for a 1.5-mile round trip. The hike described here, however, takes you past the east side of the lake, on the main trail, which continues north.

At about 1 mile the trail moves away from the lake (the upper end of the lake is marshy, and the children may want to explore a little there before they leave the area).

The trail follows below a ridge north of the lake, and there are a number of rock outcroppings that you can explore around. Remember to follow proper rattlesnake precautions by always knowing where you are stepping and never placing your hands in places you cannot see first.

The trail leads through open grassland dotted with several types of oaks. Have the children attempt to group the oaks by their leaf color, type of leaves, and type of acorns.

At about 1.25 miles the trail forks, with the left fork bending around the ridge you have been following and the right fork heading uphill back toward the parking lot. Take the right fork and continue uphill.

At about 1.5 miles the trail crosses the paved road, and then another trail. Veer to the right on the Lake Trails Loop and follow it along the ridge back toward the first small pond. If the trail is wet and muddy, you can take the paved road, for they join near the pond.

The children can explore around the many rock outcroppings that are alongside the trail on the ridge, and see if the rocks are all the same types or if there are several different types represented.

At about 2 miles you rejoin the main trail that you came uphill on. The small pond is to your right across the meadow. Take a left and head back downhill to the parking lot at 2.5 miles.

6O LAKE MARIE TRAIL

Type ■	Day hike
Difficulty ■	Moderate to difficult
Distance ■	5 miles, round trip
Hiking time ■	3 hours
Elevation gain ■	600 feet gain and loss
Hikable ■	Year-round
Map ■	Skyline Wilderness Park

Skyline Wilderness Park is one of the unique parks in the San Francisco Bay Area. While most parks are owned, operated, and financed by one or more governmental agencies, Skyline has minimal government funding and is run by the Skyline Park Citizens Association. In the 1970s this group began its quest of park status for the 850 acres and by 1978 was leasing the land from the county, which, in turn, was leasing it from the state. The land had become available in the early 1970s after the state closed part of

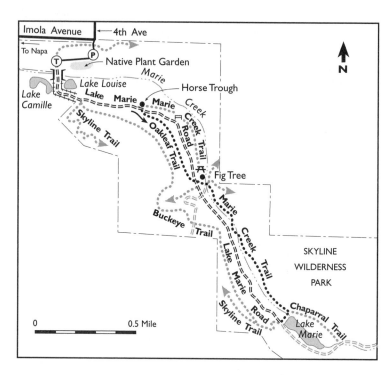

the Napa State Hospital, which for decades had used the land for various patient-operated agricultural operations.

Today the park features 17 miles of hiking on twelve trails that lead through old-growth oak woodlands, along creek banks, around lakes, and across sunny meadows dotted with wildflowers. Not really a part of the hike, but along the beginning portion of the trail, a native plant garden attracts large numbers of varied species of birds year-round. You may want to spend some time either before or after your hike strolling through the gardens and looking for birds and butterflies.

From CA 29 in Napa take Imola Avenue east to its end at Fourth Avenue. Enter the park and head to the southern corner of the parking lot. From there follow the signs to the trailhead. You will pass by the native plant garden and through a picnic area. A fenced corridor leads you between Lakes Camille and Louise before you come to a trail junction. Skyline and Buckeye Trails lead off to the right, but take a left at the fork onto Lake Marie Road, an old ranch road filled with the rounded tops of partially exposed boulders.

There is a steep climb up the road for about 0.25 mile with only minimal shade before you reach a spring-fed horse trough, where the trails head off both downhill and uphill. The Lower Marie Creek Trail is only for those with a sense of adventure, but the Oakleaf Trail that heads uphill leads through a denser oak forest and parallels the Lake Marie Road for about 0.5 mile before rejoining it. During the spring this is a good trail for wildflowers and in the summer it provides a break from the scorching sun.

If you stay on Lake Marie Road you come to a rest bench alongside the road beneath a large oak tree at 0.5 mile. From the bench you have a good view out over the lower Napa Valley, as well as of rock formations along Marie Creek.

You reach the top of a ridge at about 0.75 mile, and the road foundation becomes rockier. In fact, you begin to hike over the tops of large boulders that have been weathered to a relatively flat surface. The road descends downhill, and several trails branch off to right. At 1 mile you come to a large—nay enormous—fig tree that is estimated to be over 100 years old. A fence has been built around the tree to protect its microclimates and keep people from destroying its canopy in search of fruit. Just uphill is a fine picnic area, complete with an outhouse. The table sits under the canopy of a big oak and overlooks a meadow that has at least one grinding rock left from the days when Native Americans lived in the region. You can take a short hike downhill to Marie Creek where the children can play in the water. This is a good turnaround spot for those who don't think they will make it another 1.5 miles to the lake.

The Napa Valley spreads out before you in this view from Lake Marie Trail.

After the picnic area you enter a section of forest that has a dramatically different microclimate. This one has towering bay trees giving shadow to the trail, and alder trees line the creek downhill from the trail.

The trail continues through this lush zone until you reach the dam at 2 miles. No swimming is allowed in the lake, but the bass fishing is supposed to be good.

After a snack break you can walk across the dam, explore along the shores of the lake, or simply rest in the shade. As you head back, cross the dam and follow the signs to the Marie Creek Trail, which takes you along the opposite side of the creek through a dense bay forest and rejoins the Lake Marie Road at the picnic area near the fig tree. Retrace your route to the parking area.

61 VALLEY VIEW TRAIL

Type ▪	Day hike
Difficulty ▪	Moderate for children
Distance ▪	1.5 miles, round trip
Hiking time ▪	1 hour
Elevation gain ▪	400 feet gain and loss
Hikable ▪	Year- round
Map ▪	Westwood Hills Regional Park

In 1974 a developer proposed a 350-home subdivision on this 110-acre tract, but the city countered with a scaled-down version. When the developer balked at the new proposal, the city offered to buy the land for a park and made the purchase in 1975 for $160,000, a steal by today's standards. Today the park offers a number of short trails that lead through eucalyptus forests and across oak-studded meadows. Views from most of the trails are spectacular.

The Carolyn Parr Nature Museum is located in the park near the entrance and it is open from 1:00 P.M. to 4:00 P.M., Tuesday through Sunday. There you can see exhibits of Napa Valley plant and animal life, and pick up a trail map for the park.

From CA 29 take First Street west in Napa and continue as it becomes Browns Valley Road. The park entrance is about 1 mile

Another view of the Napa Valley, this one from Westwood Hills Regional Park.

after the road becomes Brown's Valley. The entrance is on your left.

This park has many trails for such a small park, and you can pick and choose as you like to make your own hike. The simplest is to take the Valley View Trail out of the parking lot and simply head uphill. This trail leads up a fairly steep slope through a dense eucalyptus forest, where shade is abundant. Trails begin to veer off from the main trail at about 0.25 mile, and as you reach the first flat spot

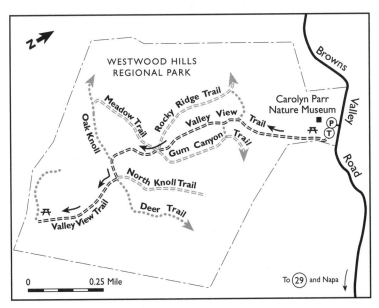

at about 0.5 mile the Rocky Ridge, Gum Canyon, and Meadow Trails all take hikers into varied parts of the park. None of these trails is more than 0.5 mile long, and all join with other trails to take you back to the Valley View Trail.

Just past this major junction the trail passes through oak-studded grassland until it ends at about 0.75 mile. There, at the high point of the park, you once had unobstructed views of downtown San Francisco and the Golden Gate Bridge to the south and of Mounts Tamalpais, Diablo, and St. Helena to the southeast, southwest, and north. Today you can still view the mountains, but a mansion with white-washed walls and red-tiled roof blocks the view of San Francisco and the Golden Gate Bridge. Even so, the views are remarkable, and the hike is pleasant.

On your way down you can make a short side-trek on the North Knoll Trail for another splendid view of the Napa Valley.

62 NAPA RIVER ECOLOGICAL RESERVE INTERPRETIVE TRAIL

Type ▪	Day hike
Difficulty ▪	Easy
Distance ▪	1.25-mile loop
Hiking time ▪	1 hour
Elevation gain ▪	Minimal
Hikable ▪	Year-round, except for wet winters
Map ▪	California Department of Fish and Game

This 73-acre preserve near the confluence of the Napa River and Conn Creek formed the southern boundary of George Yount's Rancho Caymus in 1836 and has remained virtually unchanged since that time. The eastern portion of the preserve is covered by a valley oak/bay laurel riparian forest, and is the last significant stand of such forest in the Napa Valley. The preserve is administered by the California Department of Fish and Game, and you can obtain a self-guided tour map from their Yountville office by writing to P.O. Box 47, Yountville, CA 94599, or calling 707-944-5540.

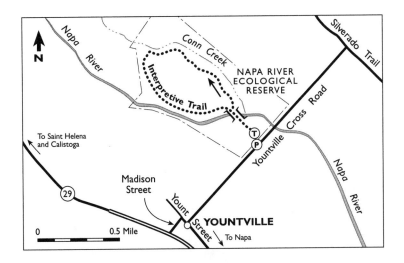

From CA 29 in Yountville go east on Madison Street for two blocks, where you turn right on Yount Street, then take a quick left on Yountville Cross Road. Go 1 mile to the small parking lot just west of the new bridge. From Silverado Trail, the main road on the east side of the Napa Valley, it is also about 1 mile to the bridge.

The parking lot sits where various church campgrounds were built in the late 1800s, and a live oak revegetation project is visible on both sides of the trail that leads toward the levee. As the trail crosses the levee, after about 100 yards it drops down into a forest of willow and sedge. Follow the trail upstream for about 50 yards to a small bridge that takes you to the east side of the river. During the winter months the bridge can be inundated, but usually is accessible when there has been little rain.

After crossing the river, a self-guided trail begins beneath an old oak. You look out over the confluence of Conn Creek and the Napa River. From the oak tree go right and begin your tour along the west bank of Conn Creek, where you may spot any one of 238 species of plants, many of which are threatened or endangered. These include Sebastopol meadowfoam, Gairdner's yampah, and pink star tulip.

As you walk along the trail you may see or hear acorn woodpeckers, rufous-sided towhees, quail, and song sparrows; volunteers have installed many bird boxes to assist species as varied as bluebirds and wood ducks.

After about 0.5 mile the trail begins to bend left toward the east bank of the Napa River. Along this portion you walk past wild plums (really feral plums from old ranching days), oaks, and huge bay trees. Poison oak, sedge, and Himalayan blackberries also abound along the trail.

As you walk along the river on the way back to the beginning of the trail, you may want to keep an eye out for fish in the clear waters. Steelhead trout are known to spawn in the river here; if you look closely you may catch a glimpse of them.

Return to the parking lot and meadow at about 1.25 miles.

The Napa River entices hikers who get a little warm.

63 REDWOOD/RITCHEY CANYON TRAILS

Type ▪	Day hike
Difficulty ▪	Difficult for children
Distance ▪	3.5 miles, round trip
Hiking time ▪	2.5 hours
Elevation gain ▪	650 feet
Hikable ▪	Year-round
Map ▪	USGS Calistoga Topographic

This 1900-acre state park is one of only two developed state parks in Napa County (Robert Louis Stevenson State Park is undeveloped except for the trail to Silverado Mine and Mount St. Helena and the Pinnacles Trail listed below), and it offers visitors camping and picnicking, as well as 10 miles of hiking trails. The park was operated as a private campground and resort known as Paradise Park for many years before the state acquired the property and developed it in 1960 as Bothe–Napa Valley State Park. This park and the adjoining Bale Grist Mill State Historic Park sit in the midst of the upper Napa Valley vineyards. The farther you go away from the campsites and the day activities of the park, the more likely you are to see some of the wildlife of Bothe–Napa Valley State Park. Raccoons, gray squirrels, deer, fox, bobcats,

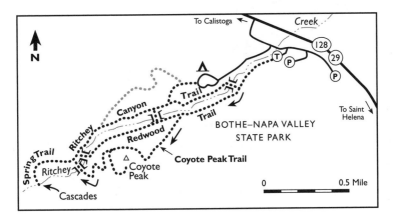

and coyote all live in the canyons of Ritchey Creek, along with six different kinds of woodpeckers, including the spectacular pileolated woodpecker.

Take CA 29 north of St. Helena for 4 miles. Turn left into the park entrance.

Ritchey Canyon Trail begins at the horse trailer parking lot and heads west up Ritchey Creek. It skirts the south side of the creek opposite the Ritchey Creek Campground. Just beyond 0.25 mile, the Ritchey Canyon Trail forks off to the right and crosses the creek. The Redwood Trail forks to the left. Take this left fork along the creek bank through a forest of large redwood and fir. The trail passes a drinking fountain—where you can quench your thirst—then climbs along the creek, and after about 100 yards passes by a small waterfall that cascades over a concrete dam.

A dizzying view skyward among the redwoods.

Just past the large buckeye tree on the right the trail forks. The right fork leads to the campground and the Ritchey Canyon Trail on the other side of the creek. Continue straight on Redwood Trail as it climbs gently to the southwest. As the trail levels out, there is a large fir on the left that has large conks, fruiting bodies of a fungus that eats the tree from the inside.

Around 0.5 mile, the redwoods thin out, and at the top of the hill at 0.75 mile all trees give way to open grassland and chaparral. As you reach the top of the next hill, the Coyote Peak Trail leads off to the left. (If you wish to cut the hike short, continue on the Redwood Trail about 100 yards past the junction with the Coyote Peak Trail, cross over the creek on a footbridge, and return to the trailhead along the Ritchey Canyon Trail on the opposite side of the creek.)

The Coyote Peak Trail leads through most of the plant communities of the park as it climbs from 500 feet to 1170 feet at the top of Coyote Peak. The north slope is forested with a heavy understory. The trail also offers views up Ritchey Canyon as it follows the contour of Coyote Peak.

At 1.25 miles take the spur trail that leads off to the left to the peak. At the peak you can rest and enjoy the views before heading back down.

Return to the Coyote Peak Trail and turn left to head down the steep slopes through chaparral on the more exposed west slope before joining with the Spring Trail at 1.75 miles. Coyote Peak, Redwood, Spring, and Ritchey Canyon Trails all join just past Ritchey Creek, where you take a footbridge across the creek. During a wet winter this may be impassable. If so, follow the creek downhill for several hundred feet to the Redwood Trail and return by that route to the parking area.

Just over the creek at the junction of the Coyote, Redwood, Spring, and Ritchey Canyon Trails take a left turn and head up the canyon. The trail climbs away from the creek until you are about 100 feet above it. The trail levels and drops back down to the creek at 1.75 miles.

You can ford the creek here to reach a side stream cascading down over moss-covered rocks. This is an excellent site for a rest stop and lunch before you head back down the trail. For a slightly different look at the creek you can return by the Ritchey Canyon Trail on the north side of the creek.

64 TABLE ROCK TRAIL

Type ▪	Day hike
Difficulty ▪	Moderate to difficult for children
Distance ▪	5 miles, round trip
Hiking time ▪	4 hours
Elevation gain ▪	800 feet gain and loss
Hikable ▪	Year-round
Map ▪	USGS Deter Reservoir Topographic

In the first edition of this guide I included a torturous 10-mile round-trip hike to the top of Mount St. Helena, where hikers can look out from the highest peak in the San Francisco Bay Area. Many people still choose to take that hike. Many younger children (not to mention their parents), however, find this hike too strenuous. In the past decade the new Table Rock Trail has been opened near Mount St. Helena. It is almost as scenic—and

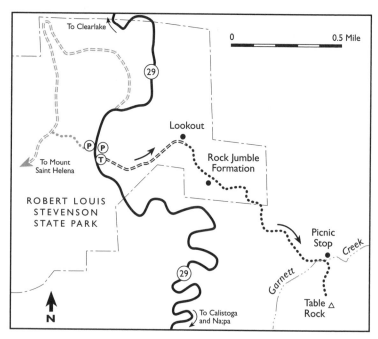

certainly less demanding. Table Rock Trail leads out from the parking lot across CA 29 from the Mount St. Helena trailhead. This trail winds through forests of tanoak, Douglas-fir, and madrone, to chaparral-covered slopes where manzanita is the dominant plant, and onto volcanic outcroppings with excellent views of the northern end of the Napa Valley.

Take CA 29 from Calistoga to Robert Louis Stevenson State Park at the summit near Mount St. Helena. Park on the east side of the highway. The trail leads out from the south side of the lot.

This hike is part of an 11-mile-long trail that takes you past Table Rock to the Palisades and the Oat Hill Mine Trails that continue down the ridge to the Silverado Trail near Calistoga. We will only go to Table Rock, however, and return by the same trail.

A manzanita struggles to survive.

The hike begins with a series of short switchbacks that take you up a steady climb through shaded forest for about 200 yards. There the trail takes a left onto a fire road, where the view soon opens up onto Snow Mountain to the north. The green slopes of the mountains offer a dramatic view in contrast to the brown hillsides that are so common in the San Francisco Bay Area during most of the year. At about 0.5 mile a flat section of hillside extends away from the trail. You can take a short break here to take in the view to the north and eat a quick snack.

Return to the trail and continue uphill. The trail offers views to the south at times along this section, and you soon enter chaparral-covered hillsides dominated by manzanita. Study this shrub as you hike by; feel its dense, heavy wood that is always cooler than the surrounding air and taste its small, applelike fruit. Native Americans and early explorers used this fruit as a staple during lean periods, but you can see how much work you must expend to get a minimum amount of food.

The road turns into a single-track trail just before 1 mile and takes a sharp right turn. Ahead of you is a beautiful rock formation where the children can play while you rest. Watch for rattlesnakes, though, and remind everyone to look before placing their hands in any crevices or on top of any rocks.

 If you look down the trail toward Table Rock and think you might not be able to make it back out, this is a good turnaround. After snacking you can simply return to the parking lot for a good 2-mile hike.

 To continue on to Table Rock head downhill through the chaparral along a trail marked by a curving row of rocks. Soon the descent becomes steeper and more treacherous as the rock-covered trail becomes loose scree. Several hikers have slipped along this section of trail in recent years and have had to be helicoptered out.

The trail continues to descend, but now through grassland until you reach Garnett Creek at 1.75 miles. This is a pretty spot for another break, and you need to collect your energy before beginning a climb up through an evergreen forest on the other side of the creek.

Soon you will come out of the forest into some great volcanic formations, and the distant ridgelines have vistas that include one that looks remarkably like a T-Rex standing guard.

At about 2 miles take a right and scramble up the volcanic tableland for a fantastic view of the Napa Valley and the Palisades below. Use extreme caution as you near the edge of Table Rock, for it drops off over 200 feet.

At Table Rock take a good nutrition break, then return to the parking lot by the same trail.

SONOMA/MARIN COUNTIES

65 CANYON/RIDGE TRAIL LOOP

Type ▪ Day hike
Difficulty ▪ Moderate for children
Distance ▪ 2.5-mile loop
Hiking time ▪ 2 hours
Elevation gain ▪ 300 feet
Hikable ▪ Year-round
Map ▪ USGS Glen Ellen Topographic

For many years Sonoma State Hospital used the 162 acres of rolling hills now included in the Sonoma Valley Regional Park as a dairy. Sonoma County acquired the land in 1973 and has developed a comprehensive trail system that crisscrosses the ridges and canyons in the park. The slopes of the canyons are studded with oaks, and wildflowers add color during the spring before the grass turns golden. The ridges offer expansive views of Glen Ellen, the Valley of the Moon, and the mountain ranges to the west and north.

Take the CA 12 exit off US 101 in Santa Rosa and continue on CA 12 for 12.5 miles east of Santa Rosa. Turn right into Sonoma Valley Regional Park.

The trail heads out of the parking lot toward two large green

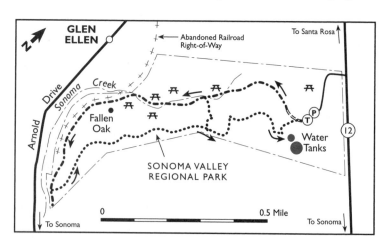

water tanks as a paved path. It turns right after about 100 yards and begins a gentle drop through open grassland that is full of poppies in the spring. A seasonal creek, which begins at a spring near a picnic area, crosses the trail a number of times.

At about 0.25 mile, the creek crosses to the left of the trail near steep slopes, but the trail continues to descend. Soon the creek recrosses the trail and there are more picnic tables beside the creek.

Oaks come in all shapes and sizes.

At 0.5 mile, a dirt trail climbs up the side of the canyon to the left; however, you should stay on the paved path as it crosses the creek again. This area is full of wildflowers as early as January, when white milkmaids bloom in abundance.

Sonoma Mountain appears in the west as the trail continues to drop, and it soon passes another picnic table near an oak draped with poison oak vines. An old Oregon oak and buckeye, bay, and live oaks are all found nearby.

The trail passes a small canyon on the left and begins to climb to a small rise as the creek moves away to the right. At 0.75 mile there is an old fallen oak and several picnic tables just before the old railroad right-of-way. The paved trail veers left and curves back to the right before it joins the right-of-way.

A grove of madrone surrounds the trail along this section as Sonoma Creek runs along the southwest side of the trail. At 1 mile a dirt trail runs parallel between the paved one and the creek, and a large manzanita bush and dozens of soap plants thrive nearby.

At about 1.25 miles the trail divides into three forks. A dirt trail leads up the hill to the left, the gravel trail veers to the left in the center, and the paved trail turns sharply to the right. The latter climbs a small hill to more picnic tables and soon comes to a gate near Arnold Drive. Those who want to take the easiest way back should simply return on the paved path. Others should take the dirt path to the left as it climbs around the end of a fence and heads northward. Large boulders lie beside the trail along this section, and wildflowers bloom beneath the scattered oak trees.

Just short of 1.75 miles, the trail takes a sharp right and begins a steep climb. At the top of the ridge the trail reaches the park boundary, bends left, and begins descending along the ridge. At the first fork the trail to the left drops abruptly back to the paved path. Continue to the right as the trail slowly descends along the fence line.

The trail soon climbs to the top of the ridge with views of the Valley of the Moon before dropping again until it becomes level at 2 miles. It climbs and drops again before coming to another fork. Stay to the right, passing views of the state hospital and Lake Suttonfield until you come to a maze of trails at 2.25 miles. Take the most used trail and continue downhill through a grove of small oaks until the trail merges with an old road. Follow the well-traveled trail to the top of the last small ridge. From there the trail descends to the green water tanks and the parking lot.

66 WOLF HOUSE RUINS TRAIL

Type ▪	Day hike
Difficulty ▪	Moderate for children
Distance ▪	1.5 miles, round trip
Hiking time ▪	1 hour
Elevation gain ▪	200 feet
Hikable ▪	Year-round
Map ▪	USGS Glen Ellen Topographic

Jack London, one of the most famous authors of the early twentieth century, moved to Beauty Ranch in Glen Ellen in 1905 when he purchased the first 127 acres. Between then and 1913 he continued to expand his holdings and began to build the home of his dreams, Wolf House. Unfortunately, the house burned just before London and his wife were to move in. London was said to never recover from this devastating loss, and the ruins stand today as they were left in 1918.

Take the CA 12 exit off US 101 in Santa Rosa and continue on CA 12 for 12 miles east of Santa Rosa. Turn left on Arnold Drive and go for not quite 1 mile to downtown Glen Ellen. As Arnold

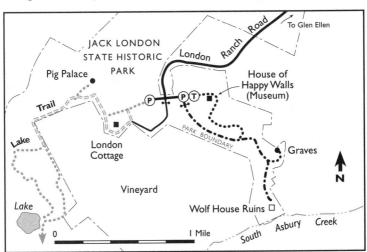

Drive takes a sharp turn to the left, London Ranch Road heads off to the right. Take this road for a little over 1 mile to the park entrance. The trail to Wolf House Ruins heads south from the front of the House of Happy Walls, which was built by London's widow, Charmain, and now houses a small museum and the park's visitor center.

The gravel trail leads past an exhibit of farm equipment that was used at Beauty Ranch, then turns left as it descends through a mixed forest with buckeye, madrone, oak, bay, and some young fir. The trail levels out at about 0.25 mile and travels along the edge of a meadow filled with poppies, Indian paintbrush, and buttercups in the spring.

At the end of the meadow, the trail crosses a small creek and climbs for a short distance before it drops again and comes to another creek. You can use the rest bench and drinking fountain here.

The trail crosses another creek and comes to a broad, paved path at just under 0.5 mile. Shortly you will come to a junction with

A close-up view of Wolf House ruins

another bench and drinking fountain. Veer to the right, where the trail drops gently as it leads along the edge of a grassy hillside with old fruit trees on the right. On the left is a stand of live and black oaks.

The trail drops more abruptly as you approach the Wolf House ruins at 0.75 mile. The ruins are surrounded by a grove of redwood trees and stand high above the banks of Asbury Creek. Have your children read *The Call of the Wild?* If so, have them guess why London called his house "Wolf House."

A trail leads you around the ruins, and there are some benches and a drinking fountain near the east side of the ruins.

As you retrace your steps back uphill, take a right at the first junction. This short spur trail takes you to London's gravesite, where a large red lava marker stands.

Return to the main trail and continue to the junction with the dirt trail you descended from the House of Happy Walls. Here you may return the way you came or continue up the paved path to the parking lot.

67 ROUGH GO/SPRING CREEK TRAILS LOOP

Type ▪	Day hike
Difficulty ▪	Difficult for children
Distance ▪	4.5-mile loop
Hiking time ▪	3 hours
Elevation gain ▪	700 feet
Hikable ▪	Year-round
Map ▪	USGS Santa Rosa Topographic

Dozens of trails that total more than 40 miles cross the 5000 acres of Annadel State Park. This state park was formed after Santa Rosa residents realized that residential developments were likely to encroach on the rolling hills that had been used for a number of years as a hiking and picnic site by the public even though it was privately owned. By 1971 Sonoma County residents had raised over a million dollars to match state and federal funding. Since then the park has become a favorite destination of hikers, horseback riders, and mountain bikers, all of whom use the trails for their individual purposes. Hikers can head to 26-acre Lake Ilsanjo for a picnic or swim, to Ledson Marsh for bird watching, or simply to the woodlands and meadows for an afternoon of exploring.

Take the CA 12 exit off US 101 in Santa Rosa and continue on CA 12 to Farmers Lane. The freeway ends here, but continue across Farmers Lane. This becomes Hoen Avenue. Continue on Hoen until you reach Summerfield Road. Cross Summerfield, where Hoen becomes Newanga Drive. Go straight to the park entrance. Continue past the base of the dam to the parking lot. From the parking lot, walk down the paved road toward the swimming area; the nature trail is on the right. Read the map and plant guide at the head of the trail and then take the short walk to the south end of the trail. From there you can join Spring Creek Trail to the south of the horse trailer parking area.

Spring Creek Trail is a broad gravel trail that parallels Spring Creek across a grassy meadow. Keep to the left at the first junction and cross a bridge at about 0.5 mile. Rough Go Trail heads to the left just past the bridge. The trail climbs steadily through scattered groves of coast live oak and black oaks. The grassland here is full of color during the spring as vetch, lupine, buttercups, and poppies all bloom.

Keep to the marked trails, although there are several unmarked spurs that lead off on both sides of the trail. Rough Go Trail makes sharp turns to the left and right as it continues its steady climb, passing some large boulders at 1 mile. This is a good place to take a rest or explore.

The trail continues to climb steadily, and just beyond the boulders there is a panoramic vista of Spring Creek Canyon. In the next 0.5 mile, you pass two trails coming in from the left and reach the crest of the hill at the second one.

From 1.5 miles to just under 2 miles, Rough Go is relatively level and offers views of Mount St. Helena to the northeast and False Lake Meadow, where wildflowers add colorful blooms during the spring.

Just before the 2-mile mark there is a trail junction with six trails heading off in various directions. Three of these are unmarked. Continue on Rough Go, which is marked, and climb south above a large meadow, over which you can see Hood Mountain.

The trail begins to descend just after 2 miles, heading toward Lake Ilsanjo. Soon the trail takes a sharp left turn and the lake is

A walk among the cattails

right in front of you.

There are picnic tables and toilets, but no water, beside the dam. You can lunch or rest while overlooking the lake, which generally has plenty of waterfowl feeding in the tules around the shore.

The Spring Creek Trail joins Rough Go Trail just before the dam. Take a right at the junction and head back toward the trailhead. This trail has much more shade than Rough Go and is a pleasure on warm days when the afternoon sun can be enervating on the more exposed trails. During the spring, shade-loving wildflowers are found under the oak canopy, and ferns grow along the creek.

The trail makes a gradual descent, and an occasional vista to the north and west is available through openings in the forest. At places where the trail comes closer to the creek, let the children explore the creekside during a rest stop.

At about 3.75 miles (1.75 from the lake), Spring Canyon Trail enters from the left, and at about 4 miles Spring Creek Trail joins Rough Go. From there return to the parking area.

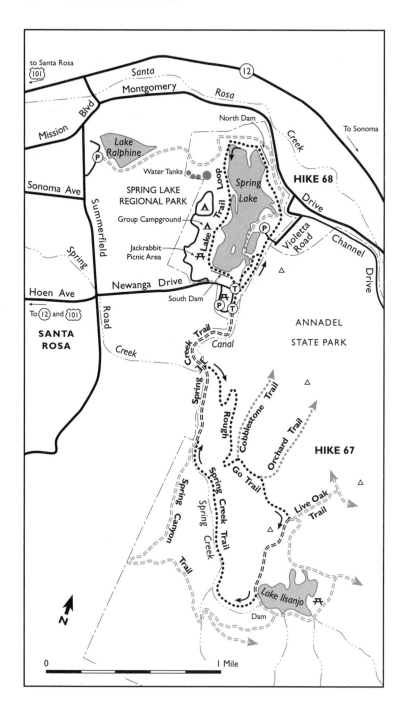

68 LAKE TRAIL LOOP

Type ▪	Day hike
Difficulty ▪	Moderate for children
Distance ▪	2.5-mile loop
Hiking time ▪	1.5 hours
Elevation gain ▪	Minimal
Hikable ▪	Year-round
Map ▪	USGS Santa Rosa Topographic
	See page 210 for Hike 68 map

Spring Lake is an artificial lake set among the oak and open grassland of the rolling hills to the east of Santa Rosa. The lake is regularly stocked with trout, and it has bass and bluegill that are easily caught by youngsters and oldsters alike. Fishing is far from the only attraction of the lake and the surrounding park, however; the swimming lagoon on the east side of the lake is popular with families during hot summers. The trails around the lake also offer a variety of hikes that the whole family can enjoy. While many are paved with asphalt and are accessible year-round—even during the rainy season, others are dirt trails that take you to sections of the lake shore that feel isolated even if they aren't.

Follow the driving directions for Hike 67 (Rough Go/Spring Creek Trails Loop). From the parking lot, cross the road and Spring Creek overflow channel to the dirt trail that heads northeast toward the lake. At the first fork take a right (the left takes you to the swimming lagoon) and another right at the second fork. This trail takes you into the edge of an oak forest uphill from the lake. Stay on the narrow footpath that parallels a wider path frequently used by horseback riders and bicyclists.

At about 0.25 mile the trail begins a series of short ups and downs as it passes through underbrush of poison oak, toyon, and berries. The trees here are mostly oaks, with some madrone and buckeye, both of which bloom with showy flowers during the spring. The buckeyes are related to the chestnut, and they have large, hard brown seedpods in the late summer and fall.

The next junction is with a trail that leads downhill toward the lake, but stay on the upper trail, which offers views of the lake and

An early morning hike around the lake provides a hazy view.

lagoon. As you come to the next junction, take a left (the right fork goes to the Shady Oak Picnic Area) and cross the paved road. Turn north toward the dam.

The vegetation here includes tall stands of fennel, thickets of berry vines, and dense coyote brush. The trail passes a solitary cottonwood at about 0.5 mile and joins a paved path that leads across an inlet of the lake. After crossing the inlet the trail again becomes dirt and follows along the shore through cottonwood, alder, and willow. The paved path runs across the top of the dam above, but it is more interesting to stay on the lower dirt path if it is not too wet. The shoreline is covered with tules, horsetail ferns, and other water plants that are home to many small birds and water animals.

At about 1 mile, near the end of the dam, the trail forks. Stay to the left along the shore of the lake. About 200 yards past the end of the dam, a faint trail leads off to the right and heads toward Lake Ralphine in Howarth Park. Go straight along the shore of the lake and head toward the end of the West Dam of Spring Lake, which is reached at 1.25 miles into the hike.

The trail becomes gravel at the end of the dam and soon veers right past several large water tanks. Follow the horse trail signs and turn away from the tanks. As you pass a cinder block building, the trail becomes somewhat unclear, but veer to your right on the gravel road for another 100 yards to more horse trail signs. The trail follows beside a chain link fence for a while before turning back into oaks where there are plenty of wildflowers during the spring.

Near 1.75 miles the trail crosses a paved road, heads through a rocky area, and merges with another trail near the Jackrabbit Picnic Area. Continue south, parallel to the paved road past the boat ramp.

At 2 miles near the Group Camping Area the path forks. Take the trail to the left across the dam to reach the parking area.

69 RAGLE RANCH TRAIL LOOP

Type ■	Day hike
Difficulty ■	Moderate for children
Distance ■	2-mile loop
Hiking time ■	1 hour
Elevation gain ■	100 feet
Hikable ■	Year-round
Map ■	USGS Sebastopol Topographic

Ragle Ranch Regional Park has the appearance of any well-groomed suburban park with its green lawns and playing fields, but there is more to the park than that. Behind the green facade lies an undeveloped region, where hikers can explore wetlands and riparian habitats that are home to dozens of species of birds. Signs of coyote, badger, raccoon, and opossum can also be found along the trail as it crosses open grassland, oak woodland, and creekside growth. The latter provides both home and food for much of the wildlife.

Take the CA 116 exit off US 101 and continue to downtown Sebastopol. Turn west on Bodega Avenue, go just over a mile to Ragle Road, and turn right; the park entrance is 0.5 mile on the left. Park at the first parking area. The trail begins at the green gate along the fence to the west of the gazebo.

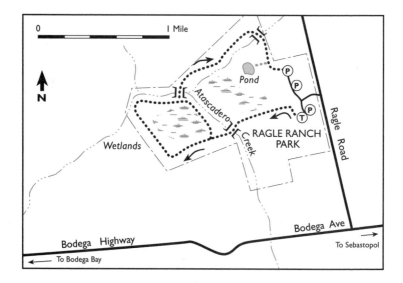

Pass through the gate and head downhill through an old orchard area. This section is home to many field birds such as the meadow-lark, and various raptors soar overhead.

At about 0.25 mile, you reach an area that is very muddy in the winter after the rains, with a small bridge that crosses the worst of the wetland. Several hundred yards past the first footbridge is Atascadero Creek, which is crossed by a larger bridge. This creek often dries up by the end of summer, but the thick growth on its banks creates wonderful places for children to explore.

The trail splits just after the bridge, with one fork going to the right and one straight ahead. The one to the right follows the creek and cuts about 0.5 mile off your hike.

Continue straight ahead and come to another wet area with a large grove of weeping willow on the left. The limbs grow close to the ground and form a canopy that your children can play under. The trail continues around the western boundary of the park, cir-cling a large meadow that becomes soggy in the wet season. At about 1 mile the trail begins to descend gently and enters a small grove of oak.

About 200 yards past the oaks the trail approaches the banks of Atascadero Creek in another wet area. Several openings in the dense brush allow access to the creek along here. At 1.25 miles you come to a normally dry tributary of Atascadero Creek that drains

Ducks eating duckweed

the vast meadow. This can be a wet crossing after heavy rains, but generally it is possible to cross without getting wet.

The trail rejoins the right fork at 1.5 miles and turns left over another bridge across Atascadero Creek. It veers to the right as it approaches a vineyard and passes a grove of eucalyptus on the left. Scattered oaks grow above the edge of the wetlands along this section, which is a wintering site for waterfowl.

There are more access points to the creek along this section of the trail, and you come to another bridge at a little over 1.75 miles. As you cross over the bridge, look closely on your right and you will see a lightly used trail that leads into the trees. A small pond just a few yards off the trail is home to a multitude of small water animals during the wet season, and it makes an excellent hidden picnic area in the summer.

The trail soon comes to another green gate. Pass through it and head up the paved road to the parking lot.

70 PIONEER/EAST RIDGE TRAILS LOOP

Type ■	Day hike
Difficulty ■	Moderate for children
Distance ■	3-mile loop
Hiking time ■	2 hours
Elevation gain ■	400 feet
Hikable ■	Year-round
Map ■	USGS Guerneville Topographic

Redwoods are awe-inspiring trees that stand high above all else, and groves of virgin trees are few in northern California. The wood in the large old trees was just too valuable for most lumbermen to ignore. But this grove of virgin trees in Armstrong Redwoods State Reserve was saved through the efforts of one investor and lumberman, Colonel James Armstrong, who came to California in 1874 to invest in the lumber industry. He became enthralled with the ancient grove of giants along Fife Creek just north of Guerneville and attempted to save them from destruction. Even after his death in 1900, his family pursued his work, and in 1917 the grove became a county park. The state parks system acquired

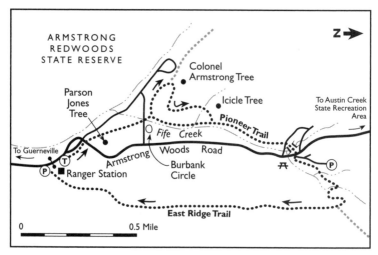

the land in 1934, and today it is one of the foremost groves of virgin trees in the lower Redwood Empire region.

Take the CA 116 exit off US 101 at Cotati and head west through Sebastopol, continuing another 16 miles to Guerneville. Head straight at the four-way stop in Guerneville and go another 2.2 miles to the park entrance. Park there and walk in.

The Southern Pomo Indian tribe had many villages in the region surrounding Armstrong Grove but avoided the grove of redwoods, which they called "the dark hole." They thought that dark, damp, and evil spirits inhabited the cool forest. Today visitors come to the grove to experience the primeval and untamed feelings that emanate from the silent surroundings. The tall trees, rushing torrents of water in midwinter, and the muted colors of wildflowers in spring all help hikers gain this experience.

From the park entrance begin your hike along the main road into the park, and veer left after about 200 yards. The trail passes the Parson Jones Tree, which at 310 feet is the tallest tree in the grove, and turns to the right after about 75 feet. Numbered posts along the trail are keyed to a nature guide that you can pick up at park headquarters.

The trail continues through a mixed redwood and fir forest that

A family hikes among the redwoods.

includes bay, tanoak, and big-leaf maple. At just less than 0.5 mile, the giant Colonel Armstrong Tree (just a couple of feet shorter than the Parson Jones Tree) stands out ahead of you. With a diameter of almost 15 feet, this is the most massive tree in the park.

A large number of old redwood trees along this stretch of trail have large caverns at their bases formed by scars left from long-ago fires. Children love to play in these and pretend they are trolls and other mythical forest creatures.

To continue the longer loop, turn left and keep along the trail beside the creek. After crossing several small bridges, you will come to the picnic area at 1 mile. This is a good place to rest and snack.

Past the picnic area veer right on the paved road and veer right again on a paved trail. You will soon come to rest rooms and a parking lot. At the east end of the parking lot head up the East Ridge Trail.

For the next 0.5 mile, the trail climbs up switchbacks through a mixed forest to a junction at the top of the ridge. Take the right fork and hike along the ridge, where you will notice the difference in vegetation because the shallow soil here supports mostly hardwoods with an occasional Douglas-fir. The trail goes up and down along this section, with views over the redwood grove to the left.

At about 2.25 miles the trail begins a steep descent of the west slope of the ridge and soon re-enters the redwood forest below. The trail leads through smaller redwoods with thick batches of huckleberry.

At about 3 miles you reach the parking lot.

71 BODEGA HEAD LOOP

Type ▪	Day hike
Difficulty ▪	Moderate for children
Distance ▪	2-mile loop
Hiking time ▪	1.5 hours
Elevation gain ▪	300 feet
Hikable ▪	Year-round
Map ▪	USGS Bodega Head Topographic

The San Andreas Fault cuts in from the Pacific Ocean to cross under land just to the east of Bodega Head. It was at this site that

Don't stray too close to the edge of seaside cliffs.

Pacific Gas & Electric decided to build a nuclear power plant in the 1950s. Environmentalists and others concerned with the safety of a nuclear plant sitting directly over a major earthquake fault successfully stopped construction of the plant, but only after the utility had dug a large hole that now sits full of spring water. The headlands are now part of the Sonoma Coast State Beach system. This narrow point of land juts out into the ocean and is exposed to the severe winds and rain that often hit the coast during the winter. As a result, there is little growth on the head other than low coastal scrub and grasses. These are, however, home to many small birds, and wildflowers bloom profusely in the open

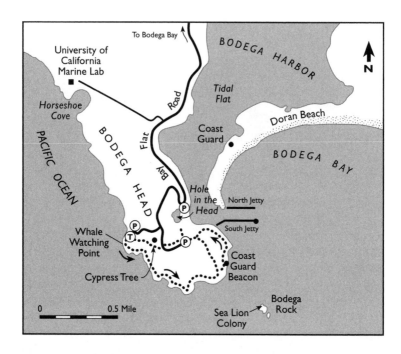

areas from February through June. Whale watching from the cliffs overlooking the ocean is also a favorite pastime during the fall and spring migration of the gray whale.

Driving north from Bodega Bay on CA 1, turn left on Bay Flat Road. Continue on Bay Flat for 4 miles to the west parking lot at the top of Bodega Head.

From the west parking lot, head toward the ocean and the wind-swept sandstone cliffs that offer some of the best whale watching along the Pacific Coast. The cliffs along the headlands are danger-ous because they are crumbly and unstable. No one should attempt to climb on them or walk along the extreme edge.

Climb over the large logs that mark the limit of the parking lot and head in a general southerly direction. The trail leads you around the edge of a small cove, with a pocket beach that is inaccessible. The kelp beds here often offer sanctuary to sea lions and harbor seals because they feed on the small marine animals that live in the kelp forests.

A lonely, gnarled cypress stands sentinel in the middle of the open grassland just in from the cliffs at about 0.25 mile. The trail along this portion moves away from the edge and broadens. This is especially welcome for those who fear heights or have overeager children.

At about 0.5 mile several inviting ledges offer good overlooks for the rocks that jut up from the surf below. Use extreme caution when walking out to them, however, because the sandstone cliffs have a tendency to create overhangs as the wind and rain sculpt them. With the added weight of hikers these can break off without warning. All along this trail section wildflowers bloom during the spring; consider bringing along a Pacific Coast wildflower guide to help you identify the many blooming plants.

For the next 0.5 mile, the trail reaches the southern point of the headlands, and you can view the entrance to Tomales Bay and Point Reyes to the south. The plant cover here begins to turn to coastal scrub from open grassland, and the low-lying wildflowers of the open grassland give way to bushy stands of blue and yellow lupine.

The trail continues along the edge of the cliffs through coastal scrub, and at about 0.75 mile a small island appears off the shore to the south. This is the home of many sea lions, whose barks echo off the cliffs most days. If you have binoculars this is a good spot to stop for a rest and observe the antics of the sea lions as they alternately sun and swim. Have your children imitate the barking sea lions; maybe they will even get a response. Have them watch as two or more sea lions try to occupy a choice, sunny spot on the rocks, and ask them to guess which one will be the winner of the ensuing struggle.

Just past the spot where you observe the sea lions is a large Coast Guard beacon. A number of trails split off soon after it. Most lead off to the left and take you back over the ridge to the east parking lot above the "Hole in the Head." If you continue straight ahead, you will follow the contour of the headlands around on an ill-defined trail that offers good views of Bodega Bay, its breakwater, and the Bodega Harbor subdivision. This trail also ends up at the east parking lot.

After a side trip of about 100 yards to view the duck pond that was meant to be the foundation pit for the nuclear power plant, continue through the east parking lot to the trail, which is easily seen as it crosses the open grassland toward the cypress tree mentioned earlier.

You may want to stop and let the children explore the sheltered cave formed by the intertwined branches of the windswept tree. On windy days it provides a good shelter for picnickers. The trail continues back to the west parking lot.

72 **TRAIL LOOP**

Type ▪	Day hike
Difficulty ▪	Moderate for children
Distance ▪	2-mile loop
Hiking time ▪	2 hours
Elevation gain ▪	400 feet
Hikable ▪	Year-round
Map ▪	USGS Petaluma Topographic

Sonoma County officials have made a concerted effort to develop a series of regional parks that help preserve at least small segments of the natural environment, as urbanization has encroached on what was until recently a rural, agricultural county. Helen Putnam County Park is one of those parks, and it is located just north of the Marin-Sonoma County line outside Petaluma. The land in the park is typical of southern Sonoma County—rolling to steep grass-covered hills with oak woodlands—and offers a number of walks within its 200-plus acres. Views are excellent on

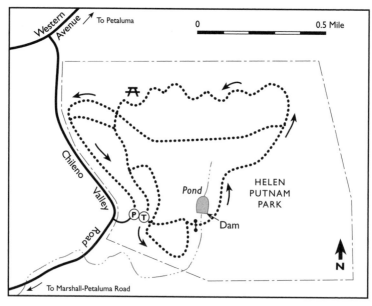

clear days, and wildflowers cover the hillsides during the spring.

Take the Washington Street exit off US 101 in Petaluma. Continue west toward the center of town and turn left on Petaluma Boulevard. Take the first right, Western Avenue, and go about 2 miles to Chileno Valley Road. Turn left on Chileno Valley and go for just less than 1 mile to the park entrance.

The trail begins about 150 feet along the paved service road from the parking area near the rest rooms, where there is a large map of the park. Head left on the trail from the map and turn right at the first redwood post marked with an arrow. The first half of the trail is marked with these posts.

The trail descends gently just past the first marker, and you duck under the limb of an old oak as you begin to climb out of the gully. From here you climb into open grassland dotted with oaks. The trail levels out at about 0.25 mile and overlooks an old ranch that is outside the park boundaries. Soon afterward the trail merges with a broader one, goes through a gate, and comes to a small pond. This is a good place to stop and explore. Your children can look for frogs and small fish among the cattails and tules that grow along the shore of the pond. They can also see how many types of dragonflies they can find among the plants. There should be blue, green, and black ones.

$\boxed{e}$

As you leave the pond, cross the dam and turn left on the paved path that follows the shore of the pond. Along this section of the trail wildflowers such as daffodils, poppies, and lupine cover the open land between the pond and the trail during the spring and early summer.

Past the pond, angle right on the path where oaks grow along the park boundary. Continue uphill until you pass through a fence and come to a multitude of trails. One on the left is marked with a redwood post. Take that one and climb for about 200 feet. Take a lightly traveled trail off to the right, where it comes close to the paved path before turning left to follow the line of oaks. It soon enters the oak forest and follows the contour of the hillside.

The scenery along this section ranges from the subdivisions of Petaluma to views of Mount St. Helena and Sonoma Mountain.

A large California buckeye stands alongside the trail, and various wildflowers such as mariposa lily and brodiaea can be seen during the spring. Unfortunately, poison oak also grows in profusion along several sections of the trail.

Just before 1 mile the trail dips and then climbs to offer fantastic views to the north. Mount St. Helena, Sonoma Mountain, and Bennett Mountain all stand out on clear days as the steam plumes from the geysers remind you of the volcanic origin of all the peaks. A small open meadow surrounded by oaks is often the site of feeding deer in early morning and evening.

At 1 mile there is a short, steep climb to the ridge, and there you will find picnic tables with views of Sonoma and Marin County hills.

The trail turns south after the picnic tables and comes to a junction of several trails after another 200 yards. Take the far right trail, which leads to the ridge after a short climb. There you are at the park boundary. The trail begins to descend to the left and then it forks. The right fork would take you along the steep boundary trail back to the parking area; instead take the left fork, which leads you along a gentler hike. It descends, crosses a broad path, and then climbs uphill again, all in about 200 yards. It then meets another well-traveled path. Turn right on this trail and climb for a short distance to the ridge. The trail splits again as you begin your descent. Take the left fork that gradually descends into a small oak-filled canyon. At the next trail junction turn right and head down the canyon to the south.

From there the trail crosses open grasslands back to the trailhead.

Watch out for slithery creatures, such as this California king snake.

73 RESERVOIR TRAIL LOOP

Type	▪ Day hike
Difficulty	▪ Moderate for children
Distance	▪ 2.5-mile loop
Hiking time	▪ 2 hours
Elevation gain	▪ Minimal
Hikable	▪ Year-round
Map	▪ USGS Petaluma Topographic

Olompali State Historic Park is one of the newer state park units in the North Bay, and it has both historical and natural features that make it a worthwhile visit. Native Americans used the site for hundreds of years for a large village, and it is even debated that Sir Francis Drake may have visited because a silver sixpence coin was uncovered during a 1974 excavation. It includes Burdell Mountain, one of the highest spots in northern Marin County, and pleasant short hikes near the historic area.

The park is located on the west side of US 101 north of Novato. Entry into the park is simple for those heading south; the entrance is well marked and requires only a right turn off the freeway. Those heading north, however, must continue past the park for about 2.5

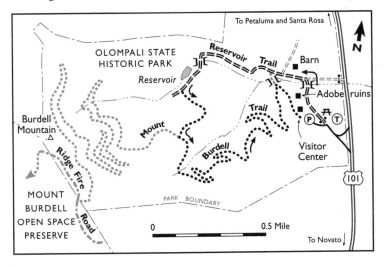

miles to the San Antonio Road exit off US 101. Instead of turning left onto San Antonio, use the exit to make a U-turn, which is legal at this particular turn. Head back south to the park entrance.

From the rear of the parking lot, follow the gravel road north. It takes you along a pomegranate hedge that protects the remains of a once-spectacular formal garden. The hedge is full of pink and white flowers during the spring. The pomegranates seldom produce fruit in this climate, but if they do happen to have fruit, they should not be picked.

You soon cross a bridge to the north side of the creek and turn left along a fire road. At about 0.5 mile, you cross back over the creek. On your right are a small reservoir and several concrete basins that were once used to water the magnificent gardens of the estate. Children will enjoy exploring around the edges of these basins for small water animals that live in the moss and algae that grow there.

You can return to the parking lot from here for a short 1-mile loop, but most will prefer to continue on the fire road past the

Search for tiny creatures around the edges of small ponds.

reservoir, and then turn left on a new trail heading up the side of the ravine.

This trail takes you uphill through areas shaded by oak, bay, and madrone, and joins the trail to the top of Burdell Mountain at about 0.75 mile. Veer to your left and continue on the trail for another 0.25 mile. The trail crosses the creek there, and this is a good spot to take a snack or picnic break.

A short distance past the creek the trail begins a fairly steep descent and includes many switchbacks as it heads back to the parking lot. It alternately leads through shaded forest and open grassland, both of which have many wildflowers in the spring.

74 DEER ISLAND TRAIL LOOP

Type ■	Day hike
Difficulty ■	Easy for children
Distance ■	1-mile loop
Hiking time ■	1 hour
Elevation gain ■	Minimal
Hikable ■	Year-round
Map ■	USGS Petaluma Topographic

This small hill was once an island surrounded by San Francisco Bay, but today stands as a sentinel in the marshlands east of Novato that were formed as the wetlands were drained. Today signs of deer, raccoon, rabbit, skunk, fox, and bobcat can all be observed on a walk around the hill.

Take the Atherton Avenue exit off US 101 and head east to Olive Avenue. Turn right on Olive and then left on Deer Island Lane. There is parking near the hill.

The trail is an easy walk around the hill, and a wide variety of wildflowers can be seen on the slopes of the hill during the spring. Huge bay and oak trees that have stood for hundreds of years cover about half the island. The other half is open grassland.

The Novato water treatment plant can be seen to the southeast of the hill, and Novato Creek's levees are to the southwest. This low-lying area is an important resting area and breeding ground for birds.

Not everyone is happy on a hike.

There are actually two trails on the hill. The first circles the base, and the second, which branches off from the first near the parking area, leads to the top of the hill and then makes a short loop back to the outer trail. Both trails offer a variety of views, and neither is strenuous.

Because it is almost impossible to get lost on this hike, older children may want to take the trail that leads to the top of the hill and hike down the other side of the island to meet those who want to hike around the perimeter of the island.

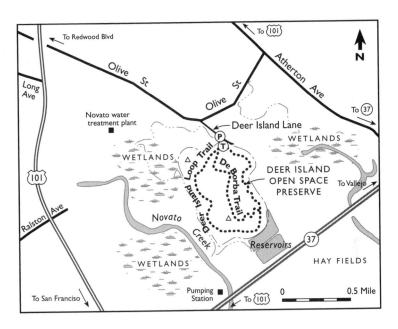

To Redwood Blvd

Olive St

Long Ave

Olive St

To (101)

Atherton Ave

To (37)

N

Novato water treatment plant ■

Deer Island Lane

WETLANDS

WETLANDS

P T

Loop Trail

De Borba Trail

Deer Island

DEER ISLAND OPEN SPACE PRESERVE

To Vallejo

101

Ralston Ave

Novato Creek

Reservoirs

37

WETLANDS

HAY FIELDS

To San Franciso

Pumping Station ■

To (101)

0   0.5 Mile

75 TOMALES BAY TRAIL

Type ■ Day hike
Difficulty ■ Moderate for children
Distance ■ 2.5 miles, round trip
Hiking time ■ 2 hours
Elevation gain ■ Minimal
Hikable ■ Year-round
Map ■ Erickson's Map of Point Reyes National Seashore, and Tomales Bay and Taylor State Parks

The 12-mile-long Tomales Bay is a submerged rift of the San Andreas Fault. The steep, wooded slopes of the Point Reyes Peninsula are typical of the Pacific Plate, and the gently rolling hills covered with grass are typical of the North American Plate. In earlier times, Tomales Bay extended southward to connect with Bolinas Lagoon, but a temporary landfill has connected Point Reyes with the mainland. This fill is marshlands that are home to

Follow the trail across pastureland to the edge of Tomales Bay.

hundreds of small animals and birds and is feeding grounds for a wide variety of shore birds and waterfowl. In 1990 the 260-acre Elmer Martinelli Ranch was purchased and made part of the Golden Gate National Recreation Area, and a 1.3-mile-long trail has been developed that crosses the ranch land from CA 1 to the bay shore.

Take CA 1 north of Point Reyes Station. A small parking lot is located on the west side of the highway, almost exactly 1 mile north of the Bank of America building in Point Reyes Station. A narrow

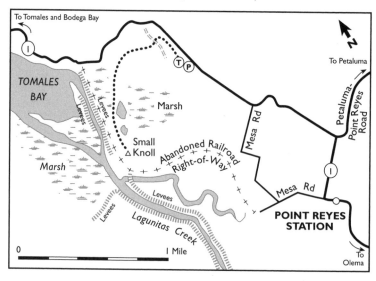

footpath is marked with a National Park Service sign and leads out from the north end of the parking lot.

The trail heads down a small draw toward a large, poison-oak-covered boulder and some boards that cross a wet stretch of the trail. From there it veers to the left and heads uphill. At the top of the ridge you have a wide-angle vista of Tomales Bay and the village of Inverness on the opposite side of the bay.

At just less than 0.5 mile, the trail crosses an old ranch road. Follow the trail markers to the left and head downhill. Two small ponds encircled by cattails and rushes that are home to red-winged blackbirds, cormorants, herons, and egrets are on the left. This is an excellent spot for kids to explore and hunt for small animals such as frogs and tadpoles.

Just past the second pond, you cross a small weir and climb uphill to reach a knoll that overlooks Tomales Bay. Ahead is a large marsh area that is active with birds and small mammals that feed in the rich marshlands.

Several long levees that cross the marsh are the remains of 12 miles of fill and trestles that carried the North Pacific Coast Railroad across the low-lying area in the early 1900s.

Return by the same route to the trailhead.

76 EARTHQUAKE TRAIL

Type ▪	Day hike
Difficulty ▪	Easy for children
Distance ▪	0.75-mile loop
Hiking time ▪	1 hour
Elevation gain ▪	Minimal
Hikable ▪	Year-round
Map ▪	Erickson's Map of Point Reyes National Seashore, and Tomales Bay and Taylor State Parks

The Point Reyes Peninsula is really an island that sits on the western side of the San Andreas Fault. The peninsula has moved northward hundreds of miles from along the Southern California coast in the past several million years. Its position along the fault

The Earthquake Trail leads past evidence that the Earth really does move.

line makes it vulnerable to seismic activity, and it was, in fact, the epicenter of the great 1906 earthquake that nearly destroyed San Francisco. There are still many visible examples of the movement along the fault at Point Reyes as a result of that quake, and Earthquake Trail near the Bear Valley Visitor Center of the Point Reyes National Seashore gives hikers an opportunity to see them.

Take CA 1 to Olema, and turn west on Bear Valley Road. The Bear Valley Visitor Center for Point Reyes National Seashore is just off Bear Valley Road, and Earthquake Trail lies to the east of the visitor center.

Earthquake Trail is a self-guided, 0.75-mile-long loop covered with asphalt. It begins at the picnic area rest rooms, across the road from the visitor center, and crosses open grassland to reach the brambles near Bear Valley Creek. The trail turns to the left and follows along between the creek and a fence that was standing at the time of the 1906 quake. At about 0.5 mile there is information, with photos and an explanation of events, about how the fence was

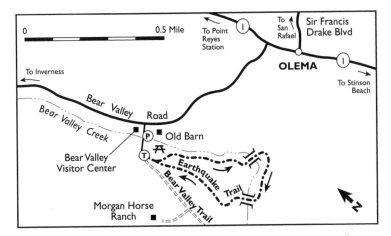

offset some 16 feet by the earth movement during the quake. Show your children the still-standing sections of fence that were offset by the quake to let them know how much 16 feet is.

The trail soon crosses back over Bear Valley Creek and heads back to the picnic area. This stretch of the trail passes by a number of large oak trees and through a wide variety of wildflowers that provide splotches of color to the green meadow from early spring to summer.

77 LIMANTOUR SPIT TRAIL

Type ■	Day hike
Difficulty ■	Easy for children
Distance ■	2 to 4 miles, round trip
Hiking time ■	3 hours
Elevation gain ■	None
Hikable ■	Year-round
Map ■	Erickson's Map of Point Reyes National Seashore, and Tomales Bay and Taylor State Parks

Limantour Spit is one of the longest sandbars on the West Coast and separates Estero de Limantour from Drakes Bay. Drakes Bay joins with Estero de Limantour at the end of Limantour Spit.

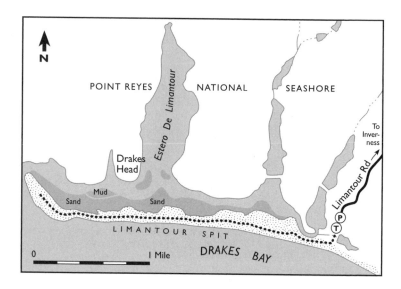

Littoral currents that parallel the shore and deposit sand at the mouths of esteros, where water is too calm to keep sand suspended, form sand spits such as Limantour. Two-mile-long Limantour has been set aside as a natural area.

From CA 1 in Olema take Bear Valley Road west to Limantour Road. Turn left and continue to the parking lot at the end of the road. A paved path leads through ponds and marshes from the parking lot to the beach.

This hike is more free-form than most of the others in this guide because there are numerous small trails that lead off the beach into the marshlands on the estero side, and the beach is open for either long or short walks.

Hikers who take some of the side trails, and/or walk all the way to the end of the spit, may hike as much as 4 miles round trip; those who stay pretty much to the center of the spit, and only go about halfway to the end, will only hike about 2 miles round trip.

Harbor seals, shorebirds, and waterfowl are all found here in abundance, and a walk along the beach or into the marshlands is a birdwatcher's dream. Even raccoon prints can frequently be spotted near the end of the spit, where grassy mounds become islands during high tide.

During weekends in the full bloom of spring the beach is crowded, but more stimulating hikes can be found during the beginning or end of winter storms when the beach becomes a wild, windswept

The wide tidal marshes of Limantour contain many types of wildlife.

refuge from civilization, and hikers have little company. Children enjoy hiking along the spit after heavy winter storms because they can find vast quantities of drift material along the beach. They like to fantasize about where the material came from and how it got in the ocean.

78 ABBOTTS LAGOON TRAIL

Type ■	Day hike
Difficulty ■	Moderate for children
Distance ■	3 miles, round trip
Hiking time ■	2 hours
Elevation gain ■	200 feet
Hikable ■	Year-round
Map ■	Erickson's Map of Point Reyes National Seashore, and Tomales Bay and Taylor State Parks

There is something haunting and lonely about the land on the ocean side of Point Reyes Peninsula, and the land around Abbotts

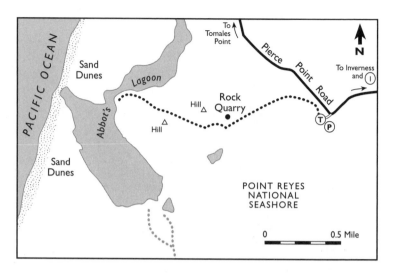

Lagoon certainly fits that description. The hills are covered with grass that is green during late winter and spring, but a dull gray the rest of the year; salt-tinged winds sweep in off the ocean; fog often hangs overhead all day; and only yellow and blue bush lupines add noticeable splotches of color to an otherwise monochrome vista. Even the water of the lagoon (actually a pair of lagoons separated by a narrow isthmus of land) takes on a gray hue on most days. With that said, this can be an invigorating hike. The air is always brisk; there are seldom any other hikers to break the solitude of the moors; and the beach is always a spot to watch shorebirds flit and feed.

Take Sir Francis Drake Highway west from CA 1 just south of Point Reyes Station for 2.5 miles to Pierce Point Road. Turn right and follow the signs to Tomales Bay State Park. Continue past the park entrance on Pierce Point Road for 1.5 miles to a small parking lot with rest rooms on the west side of the road. The trail to the lagoon leads out of the parking lot.

The hike is simple, the trail is gentle, and the view is unobstructed as you wind your way down the trail from the road to the upper reaches of the lagoon. Near the lagoon, hikers can view shorebirds and waterfowl, as well as occasional small animals. The sand dunes before the beach offer good seats for adults to contemplate or enjoy the view while the kids work off some energy by running, jumping, and sliding on the sides of the dunes. A small

Even in winter it's fun to walk along a flat beach as the waves lap at your feet.

stream drains the lagoons into a small pool at the beach, from which the water gently makes its way to the ocean. This is a good spot to take a rest or eat lunch before heading back to the parking area.

79 PIONEER TREE TRAIL LOOP

Type ■ Day hike
Difficulty ■ Moderate for children
Distance ■ 3-mile loop
Hiking time ■ 2 hours
Elevation gain ■ 200 feet
Hikable ■ Year-round
Map ■ Erickson's Map of Point Reyes National
Seashore, and Tomales Bay and Taylor
State Parks

This easily accessible hike takes you through good stands of redwood trees that have withstood the ravages of fire and disease and stand as a tribute to the indestructible qualities of the species.

Take the Sir Francis Drake Boulevard exit off US 101 and go about 16 miles west, passing the village of Lagunitas, to the signs for the Samuel P. Taylor State Park entrance. Park in the lot by the park office. Pioneer Tree Trail begins at the Redwood Grove Picnic Area. Follow the Old Railroad Grade Road from the picnic area; the Pioneer Tree Trail veers to the right just before the creek.

The trail leads over several small hills and then climbs slowly to

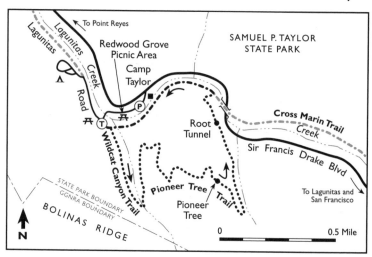

This picnic area was built courtesy of the CCC during the 1930s.

the top of a small summit that offers views of Lagunitas Creek and the park. A bench is located here (about 0.75 mile from the trailhead) for those who like to sit on something substantial after a climb.

You head downhill for the next 0.25 mile, continue past a huge fallen fir tree, and soon come to the Pioneer Tree. This ancient redwood stands in the center of a circle of offspring trees that have sprouted from its roots, and has a deep fire scar that can hold several people at one time. The next tree also has a huge scar from the same fire. This spot is a good picnic area, with several benches for facing the trees. Children love to play in the cavities formed by the fires.

The trail continues downhill for another 0.25 mile and passes through a tunnel formed by giant tree roots before reaching the fire road that was the grade for the railroad that brought tourists to Camp Taylor and Point Reyes until about 1930. The road leads back to the picnic area along Lagunitas (Paper Mill) Creek.

80 FERN CANYON TRAIL

Type ■ Day hike
Difficulty ■ Moderate for children
Distance ■ 1-mile loop
Hiking time ■ 1 hour
Elevation gain ■ 200 feet
Hikable ■ Year-round
Map ■ Erickson's Map of Point Reyes National
Seashore, and Tomales Bay and Taylor
State Parks

Point Reyes National Seashore is an outstanding example of how large tracts of near-virgin land can be set aside near major metropolitan areas for the enjoyment of all. It contains thousands of acres of untamed wilderness and features hundreds of hikes. At the southern end of the seashore is a little-known canyon of the Arroyo Hondo Creek, which drains an 8-mile-long, 8000-acre watershed. The creek runs year-round and provides the canyon with enough water to form an almost tropical ecological system. With native rainbow trout, giant salamanders, rough-skinned newts, a dozen resident bird species, and four major types of ferns, there is plenty of flora and fauna for all.

Take the Stinson Beach exit off US 101. Head north on CA 1 for

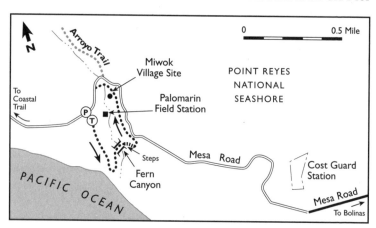

This is just one variety of fern found in Fern Canyon.

4.5 miles past Stinson Beach. At the north end of Bolinas Lagoon, the Bolinas-Fairfax Road joins CA 1. (A word of caution: this road may not be marked because Bolinas residents frequently remove the Bolinas-Fairfax Road sign to confuse tourists. But it's not hard to miss as it is the only fork at the north end of the lagoon.) Turn left onto this road and follow it for 1.25 miles on the west side of Bolinas Lagoon to Mesa Road. Turn right on Mesa and continue for about 4 miles. This takes you into the Point Reyes National Seashore, past the U.S. Coast Guard Station, and to the Palomarin Field Station of the Point Reyes Bird Observatory. Park in the lot just beyond the field station building. The Fern Canyon trailhead begins on the east side of the parking lot.

Bird banding occurs at the field station during various seasons, and a small museum at the field station describes the activities that take place there. Ornithologists are people who study birds. They study migration by catching birds, placing a small, colored leg band with information about who placed the band, and then releasing them. If these birds are later recaptured by other ornithologists, or found by nonscientists, the person who banded the bird is notified. This gives scientists much information about where and when birds travel. Children can observe birds being banded at the field station, and families can actually help with the banding by volunteering in advance.

At the field station you can pick up a small brochure, *Fern Canyon Guide*, which is not a "go-by-the-numbers" guide, but has drawings and descriptions of animals, birds, plants, and landscapes to help you locate your position on the nature trail. Have the children use the guide to track where you are.

The first part of the trail descends gently through coastal scrub, which is dotted by poles that mark study grids used by the field station.

At about 0.25 mile, the trail comes to an overlook above the edge of the woodland that covers most of Fern Canyon. The overlook is well used and is the only spot where you should leave the main trail. Any side trails you encounter are only for the use of field station researchers.

Just past the overlook the trail plunges down into the dark recesses of the canyon. There, a canopy of evergreens such as bay and oak shade the creekside and provide a glen where five-finger, polypody, lady, and sword ferns abound.

To reach the glen, or "Fern Canyon," which is about 0.5 mile from the trailhead, descend an easy-to-manage four-rung ladder. Stop and explore the many wonders to be found in such enchanted places.

To begin the final leg of the hike, you cross the creek on a footbridge and climb a series of steep steps on the opposite side of the creek. The trail then heads through a group of huge old buckeye trees, past a landslide, and to the site of an old Miwok village at Miwok Meadows. Nothing remains of the village, although it is easy to imagine how the village would have looked as the Miwok went about their daily activities.

Past the village site the trail heads out of the canyon and back into dense coast scrub. This side of the canyon is more moist, and the scrub is correspondingly greener.

The trail ends at Mesa Road, 0.75 mile from the trailhead. Turn left at the road and return to the parking lot at the field station.

81 RAWLINGS/KENT TRAILS LOOP

Type ▪ Day hike
Difficulty ▪ Moderate for children
Distance ▪ 1-mile loop
Hiking time ▪ 1 hour
Elevation gain ▪ 250 feet
Hikable ▪ March through July
Map ▪ USGS Bolinas Topographic

Although the wonderfully colorful great blue herons and great egrets can be spotted individually around the bay area, they can be seen at their finest each spring at the Audubon Canyon Ranch near Bolinas Lagoon. The great blue heron stands 4 to 5 feet tall and has a wingspan of up to 6 feet. The great egret is only slightly smaller and has outstanding breeding plumage. This plumage almost caused the extinction of the birds during the early part of the twentieth century as hunters killed them by the thousands for their beautiful feathers, which were used as ornaments for women's hats. Both of these magnificent birds build their stick

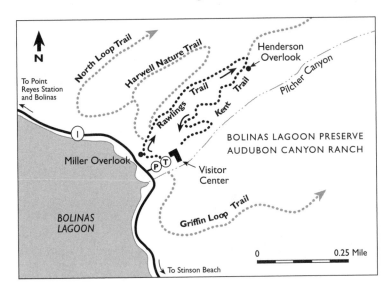

nests high in redwood trees in a large rookery in Pilcher Canyon behind the headquarters of Audubon Canyon Ranch, where they can be viewed from an overlook during breeding season. The birds are protected in the redwood forest, and they have a ready supply of food in nearby Bolinas Lagoon.

Take the Stinson Beach exit from US 101, and continue on CA 1 for 3.25 miles past Stinson Beach. Signs on the right side of the highway lead you to the parking lot at headquarters. The trail to the overlook heads uphill behind the visitor center.

The Rawlings Trail starts up the side of a ravine to the north of the visitor center, then heads through a heavily forested area with a canopy of oak, bay, and madrone. During the spring this part of the trail has many wildflowers and mushrooms.

At the first sharp U-turn at about 0.2 mile, you will find an overlook named after the late congressman Clem Miller. From a bench

Wildlife thrives in the marshes along the edges of reservoirs.

at this overlook you can watch herons, egrets, and other birds fishing in Bolinas Lagoon.

At about 0.5 mile you come to the Henderson Overlook, where you are at a slightly higher elevation than the nests in the Pilcher Canyon rookery. At the overlook, rest on one of the wooden benches and watch the constant activity of more than 120 herons and egrets as they fly from their nests to the lagoon and back. The herons begin nesting in late February and the egrets several weeks later in March. The excitement at the rookery peaks between mid-April and mid-June, when several hundred nestlings are hatched and squawk for food.

After viewing the herons and egrets return the 0.5 mile to the visitor center on the slightly steeper Kent Trail.

At the visitor center you may wish to pick up the guide to the Bert C. Harwell Nature Trail, a 1-mile loop that is just north of the Rawlings/Kent Trails Loop, and add a hike along it to this one.

Audubon Canyon Ranch is open to visitors only during the nesting season, generally March through July, on Saturdays, Sundays, and holidays from 10:00 A.M. to 4:00 P.M.

82 PHOENIX LAKE TRAIL LOOP

Type ▪	Day hike
Difficulty ▪	Easy for children
Distance ▪	1.5-mile loop
Hiking time ▪	1.5 hours
Elevation gain ▪	Minimal
Hikable ▪	Year-round
Map ▪	Rambler's Guide to Trails of Mount Tamalpais and the Marin Headlands, Olmsted & Brothers

The Marin Municipal Water District has five storage lakes on the north slope of Mount Tamalpais that supply water to Marin residents. These lakes also provide excellent hiking for families. This side of the mountain is generally cooler, shadier, wetter, and wilder than the more populated south side. Although the trails immediately adjacent to the lakes are busy, you can hike for a

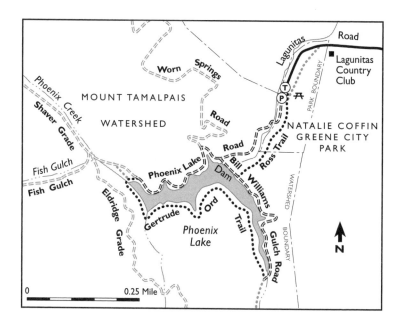

whole day on some of the outlying trails without encountering another person. Trails connect Phoenix, Lagunitas, and Bon Tempe Lakes for longer hikes.

To reach Phoenix Lake, take the Sir Francis Drake Boulevard exit off US 101. Follow Sir Francis Drake into Ross and turn left on Lagunitas Road. Follow Lagunitas to the Natalie Coffin Greene City Park parking lot. The trailhead is a short distance southwest of the parking lot.

Phoenix Lake is a small lake, and the walk around it is easy any season of the year. It offers wildflowers and nesting birds in the spring, active birds and fishing in the summer, colorful leaves in the fall, and cascading creeks in the winter.

The south side of the lake is an excellent site for ferns. Many varieties can be found there in the winter.

Because the north side and south side of the lake have such different vegetation, you may want to have the children note what types of plants (more grasses and hard brush) grow along the more exposed, dry northern shore, and compare them with those (ferns and soft brush) that grow on the protected, damp, southern shore.

For a longer hike take Fish Gulch Trail from the west end of Phoenix Lake to Lagunitas Lake. This 1-mile trail climbs just over 600 feet and takes about 1 hour. If you take the side trail to

Look for redwing blackbirds and listen for frogs in the tules and cattails.

Lagunitas Lake, you return to the Phoenix Lake Trail by the same route and continue on around Phoenix Lake to complete the loop. There is a picnic area in Natalie Coffin Greene City Park.

83 VERNA DUNSHEE TRAIL LOOP

Type ■	Day hike
Difficulty ■	Easy for children
Distance ■	1.5-mile loop
Hiking time ■	1 hour
Elevation gain ■	350 feet
Hikable ■	Year-round
Map ■	Rambler's Guide to Trails of Mount Tamalpais and the Marin Headlands, Olmsted & Brothers

Mount Tamalpais is the dominating physical feature of Marin County, and on one of the rare clear days, from East Peak you can see the snow-covered peaks of the Sierra Nevada 200 miles away.

A camera helps record the memories of great hikes.

Because of its breathtaking panoramas that include Tiburon, Mount Diablo, the Marin Headlands, the San Francisco skyline, and the Farallon Islands 26 miles out into the Pacific Ocean, Mount Tamalpais has been a popular hiking destination for San Francisco residents since the 1880s, when they had to take a ferry to reach the North Bay region.

Today Mount Tamalpais State Park offers more than 200 miles of trails that cross grass-covered hills, wander along stream banks, venture into damp redwood canyons where waterfalls flow in torrents over rocks and boulders, and break through chaparral on sun-baked slopes. The hikes described here are only a selection of many hikes you can take.

To reach the East Peak visitor center and parking lot, take CA 1 off US 101 at the Stinson Beach exit. Leave CA 1 after 3 winding miles, and turn right on Panoramic Highway. Follow the signs to Mount Tamalpais past the Muir Woods Road and Mill Valley intersection, and parking lots for Mountain Home, Bootjack, and Pantoll to Southside Road. Turn right on Southside Road and continue 1 mile to East Ridgecrest Boulevard. Turn right on Ridgecrest and go 3 miles to the parking lot.

The Verna Dunshee Trail Loop includes the best vista points on Mount Tamalpais and is an easy trek for young and old alike. Begin at the visitor center and follow the paved trail counterclockwise around the peak. At about 0.25 mile you can stop at some benches and view the East Bay and Mount Diablo, if the smog is not too thick. Continue on for several hundred yards where you cross a wooden bridge. Look up at the rocks above; you will almost always see some rock climbers scaling the granite boulders.

At just less than 0.5 mile a poorly marked trail leads off to the right to the North Knee of Mount Tamalpais, and you must grapple your way through the hard, sharp chaparral plants that cover the short ridge. Children like this side trip because it takes them away from the easily traveled trail and becomes an adventure.

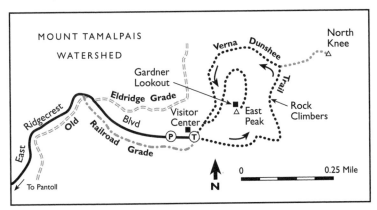

Although the trail to the North Knee is not well marked, it is easy to follow because the ridge is narrow, and you head down a steep slope if you wander away from the trail. After you reach the Knee, which juts up out of the chaparral, you return to the main trail by the same route.

As you come back to the main trail, you enter an area with larger plants and trees that offer some shade on hot days, making this a good spot to take a break.

Continue on around the peak and view the vast undeveloped, forested area owned by the Marin Municipal Water District, and two of the district's five lakes. The largest is Bon Tempe, and nearby is the smaller Lagunitas.

The Verna Dunshee Trail ends near the visitor center, but you can take a sharp left turn onto the 0.2-mile trail to the 2571-foot summit of East Peak where Gardner Lookout sits. Be forewarned before starting up this trail with your little ones that all of the 350-foot elevation gain is on this short section of the trail.

Plenty of picnic sites, rest rooms, water, and snacks are available at the visitor center.

84 STEEP RAVINE TRAIL TO STINSON BEACH

Type ▪	Day hike
Difficulty ▪	Moderate to difficult for children
Distance ▪	3–4 miles, round trip
Hiking time ▪	3 hours
Elevation loss ▪	1100 feet
Hikable ▪	Year-round
Map ▪	Rambler's Guide to Trails of Mount Tamalpais and the Marin Headlands, Olmsted & Brothers

Steep Ravine in Mount Tamalpais State Park is formed by Webb Creek and offers hikers large redwoods, waterfalls, and views of the ocean. During early spring the rushing creek cascades over numerous waterfalls, and wildflowers—particularly trillium—abound on its banks. Ferns of many kinds (sword, five-finger,

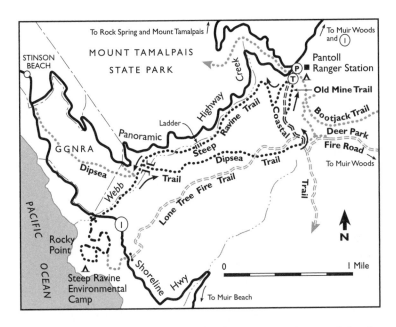

spreading wood, Woodward, and others) cover the creek banks and hang from the trees and rocks.

Follow the directions to East Peak given for Hike 83 (Verna Dunshee Trail Loop), but stop at the Pantoll Ranger Station and parking lot. A sign indicating the Steep Ravine Trail is at the south end of the parking lot.

The first 0.5 mile of the trail switches back through a forest of redwood, fir, and bay until its reaches Webb Creek and a footbridge. In the next mile you cross several footbridges, descend several steep grades by means of steps, and climb down one ladder as the creek drops precipitously down the ravine. The trail is not dangerous, but it is steep and slippery in spots. To prepare your children for the steep decline after crossing the first bridge, ask them to guess where the next bridges, steps, and ladder will be by listening for rapids in the creek during times when the water is flowing heavily, or have them look for other signs that the trail is beginning to drop more rapidly.

After 1.5 miles, the Steep Ravine Trail is joined by the Dipsea Trail, which crosses a footbridge just east of the Steep Ravine Trail.

You have several choices at this point. First, you can choose to continue on the Steep Ravine Trail for another mile to Rocky Point. To reach this windswept point, continue down the Dipsea

This ladder makes the Steep Ravine Trail passable.

Trail about 30 yards past a dam, which is 50 yards from the junction of the two trails. The Steep Ravine Trail branches off the Dipsea Trail and continues over CA 1 to Rocky Point.

Another choice is to turn back up the Dipsea Trail, continue uphill for about 1.5 miles to the Old Mine Trail, and on another 0.25 mile to the parking lot at Pantoll. This is a strenuous climb, however, so be prepared.

The third choice is to keep right on the Dipsea and head on down to the seaside town of Stinson Beach. From there you can take a Golden Gate Transit bus back to Pantoll.

Those who hike on to Rocky Point can return to the Dipsea Trail and head on into Stinson Beach, or up the Dipsea Trail to the Old Mine Trail, and back to Pantoll.

If you choose to hike to Stinson Beach to catch a bus back to Pantoll, contact the Golden Gate Transit Authority (415-455-2000) for bus schedules from Stinson Beach to Pantoll.

85 REDWOODS GROVE TRAIL LOOP

Type ▪ Day hike
Difficulty ▪ Easy for children
Distance ▪ 1-mile loop
Hiking time ▪ 1 hour
Elevation gain ▪ Level
Hikable ▪ Year-round
Map ▪ Rambler's Guide to Trails of Mount Tamalpais and the Marin Headlands, Olmsted & Brothers

Muir Woods National Monument is one of the most popular tourist attractions in Marin County and has some of the most stringent restrictions of any park in this guide: You may not ride motor vehicles, horses, or bicycles; bring pets of any kind; or even picnic within the boundaries of the monument. Is it worth a day

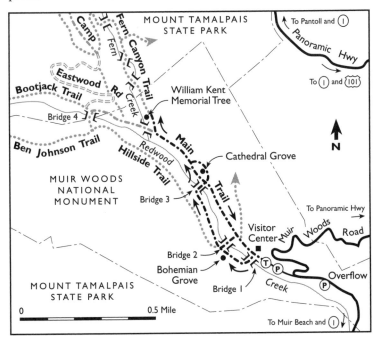

The deep shadows of Muir Woods

hike? Most assuredly, for its 580 acres contain the world's most famous redwood grove, and even on a crowded summer weekend you can find solitude away from the masses. Midweek hikes are much more enjoyable, though, for that is when the majestic redwoods, which reach up to 253 feet in the grove; the creek, which has rushing rapids complete with spawning salmon in winter and quiet pools in the summer; and the canyon, with its fern-covered sides, provide a wonderful buffer from the bustling world just across the ridge.

Take CA 1 off US 101 at the Stinson Beach exit. Continue west for 3 winding miles to Panoramic Highway; go right for 1 mile to

 Muir Woods Road. Turn left and continue 1.5 miles to the parking lot, which will resemble a shopping center parking lot on sunny weekends.

The trail from the parking lot to the visitor center passes markers pointing out the more common plants found in the redwood forests. On the west side of Redwood Creek, across from the center and accessible by a wooden bridge, is a 0.25-mile-long nature trail in Bohemian Grove. At the end of the nature trail another footbridge crosses to the east side of the creek, where you enter Cathedral Grove.

Another 0.25 mile takes you to the William Kent Memorial Tree, a 278-foot Douglas fir, which is the tallest tree in the monument. This tree is enormous by any standard, and children like to try to see how many people it takes to put their arms around it. Also have them guess how many people it would take, standing on each other's shoulders, to be as tall as the tree. You can backtrack along the east side of the creek and continue south to the visitor center, passing a memorial to Gifford Pinchot, an early conservationist.

This hike is completely within the monument so you cannot enjoy a picnic, but you can stop for a snack and a cup of coffee at the visitor center.

86 CORTE MADERA STATE ECOLOGICAL RESERVE TRAIL

Type ■	Day hike
Difficulty ■	Easy for children
Distance ■	3 miles, round trip
Hiking time ■	2 hours
Elevation gain ■	None
Hikable ■	Year-round
Map ■	USGS San Quentin Topographic

The Corte Madera State Ecological Reserve is one feature of the paved Corte Madera Creek Path that runs for 2 miles along Corte Madera Creek to San Francisco Bay. The reserve is a restored wetland; the wide, meandering creek empties into the bay.

Take the Sir Francis Drake Boulevard exit off US 101 and follow signs to the Golden Gate Ferry's Larkspur terminal. Park in the terminal parking lot.

From the terminal parking lot, head east on the path toward Remaillard Park, where the Marin Audubon Society has restored the duck pond and turtles and ducks can again be seen. Have the children search for turtles on small logs or other objects that stick

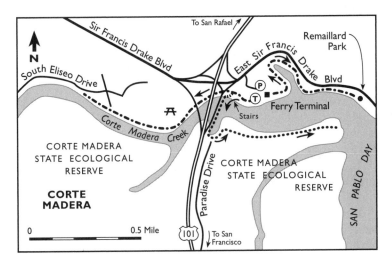

The freeway is only a stone's throw from this catwalk.

up out of the water near taller water plants. On sunny days, frogs often can be seen warming themselves, but you must be very quiet if you want to get a close-up look at them. You may also want to see how many different types of ducks are at the pond.

Circle around the pond on the dirt trail and head back to the parking lot the way you came. Continue past the parking lot and a group of false-fronted buildings just before the freeway. Just west on the path past the false-fronted buildings is a trail junction. To the left is the Corte Madera State Ecological Reserve.

To reach the reserve, leave the path and head left up the stairway to a sidewalk on the overpass. Follow Paradise Drive 0.5 mile to the reserve, then backtrack to the trail junction. Turn left under the freeway and out along the creek.

A small, grassy creekside park with picnic tables and benches located just past the freeway offers an excellent view of Mount Tamalpais as it towers over Corte Madera.

You can continue on the path along the creek for another 0.5 mile. Turn around at South Eliseo Drive and return to the ferry terminal parking lot.

87 ANGEL ISLAND TRAIL LOOP

Type ▪	Day hike
Difficulty ▪	Moderate for children
Distance ▪	5-mile loop
Hiking time ▪	4 hours
Elevation gain ▪	Minimal
Hikable ▪	Year-round
Map ▪	USGS San Francisco North Topographic

This 1-square-mile island is the largest in San Francisco Bay and has a long history: it has been a prison, an army fort, a missile base, and an immigration detention center. Today Angel Island State Park is a tranquil setting in the midst of a bustling metropolitan region.

The native flora and fauna of the island are similar to that of nearby mainland regions, but over the centuries humans have introduced a number of exotic plants. For more than a decade the state parks department has been removing some of the exotics, particularly the

Grandparents can have as much fun as their grandchildren.

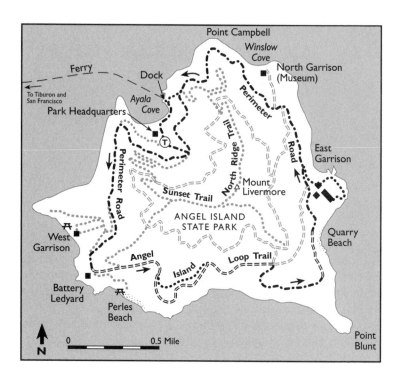

large stands of eucalyptus trees that covered the south slope of the island.

Ferries serve the island from San Francisco (415-546-2896) and Tiburon (415-435-2131). Call for current schedules because they change seasonally.

The 5-mile loop trail that circles the island is relatively flat and passes through several historical sections. It begins at park headquarters near Ayala Cove, and it has both surfaced and non-surfaced sections.

Take the road uphill from the headquarters for about 0.25 mile to Perimeter Road, which continues around the island. Various side trails lead hikers to historical sites, as well as vista points.

As you continue on Perimeter Road in a counterclockwise direction around the island, you will come to a number of historical sites. The first of these, at just over 1 mile, is Camp Reynolds, or the West Garrison. Established in 1863, this was the first military installation on the island. It was in continuous operation until 1946. A short side trail leads to the old buildings, which can be explored from the outside.

These buildings, restored to their 1880s appearance, are used for history programs. Children love to imagine what life was like for soldiers during those years as they explore the grounds where the troops drilled more than a century ago.

Return to the Perimeter Road and continue around the island. At 1.25 miles, near an old gun emplacement called Battery Ledyard, glimpse a spectacular view of San Francisco and the Golden Gate. Just past the emplacement a side trail leads off the main road for 0.25 mile down to small, sheltered Perles Beach. Children like to play in the sand here as they look for objects that have drifted ashore.

Continue on the Perimeter Road, which is now dirt, to just past 2 miles where there is a four-way junction. Take the road to the right, which becomes paved again, and after several hundred yards you are above Point Blunt, which was a favorite dueling grounds for San Franciscans in the 1800s. You overlook the point from an old Nike missile site that is not nearly as picturesque as Battery Ledyard, but still interesting historically.

The road goes downhill to about 2.5 miles, where it forks once again. Take the left fork, because the right one goes to a Coast Guard station that is off limits.

At 3 miles the road passes the East Garrison, which was built in the 1890s to house soldiers returning from the Philippines. This garrison is much less attractive and interesting than the West Garrison.

At 3.25 miles you overlook the North Garrison at Point Simpton, where an immigration station similar to Ellis Island in New York was established in 1909. There is a small museum on the history of the immigration station here that is well worth visiting. Children are intrigued by the stories of privations and challenges met by the early immigrants, most of whom were from Asia.

From the North Garrison return to the Perimeter Road and continue on past Point Campbell, the northernmost point of the island, at about 4 miles, and on back to Ayala Cove. At about 4.5 miles, the North Ridge Trail crosses Perimeter Road and heads down a series of stairs to the cove. You can choose this as a shorter, but steeper, route back to the dock. Otherwise, continue on the road back to the cove.

In addition to the historical sites, seabirds and sea mammals are a primary attraction of this trail.

88

TERWILLIGER NATURE TRAIL LOOP

Type ■ Day hike
Difficulty ■ Easy for children
Distance ■ 0.5-mile loop
Hiking time ■ 1 hour
Elevation gain ■ Minimal
Hikable ■ Year-round
Map ■ USGS San Quentin Topographic

Richardson Bay Wildlife Sanctuary is operated by the Audubon Society as an environmental education center with a nature trail and interpretive programs for groups. It includes 11 acres of land and 900 acres of water with a variety of habitats for birds, small mammals, and other bayshore animals.

Take the Tiburon/Belvedere (CA 131) exit off US 101. Continue east on Tiburon Boulevard for about 1 mile, and turn right on

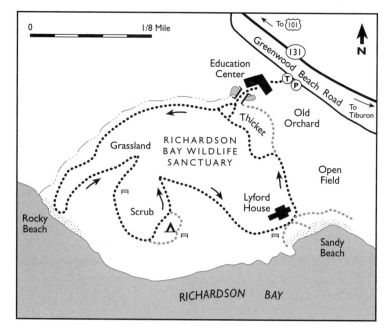

Greenwood Cove Drive. This soon becomes Greenwood Beach Road. Follow this road for 0.25 mile to the large yellow Victorian mansion on the right. Park by the education center off Greenwood Beach Road. The sanctuary is open 9:00 A.M. to 5:00 P.M., Wednesday through Sunday.

Pick up a self-guiding brochure at the education center. This gives an excellent introduction to the sanctuary's flora and fauna as seen along the nature trail.

The trail begins behind the center and immediately crosses a small pond on a footbridge. Take the trail to the right along a seasonal creek for a short hike to Rocky Beach. There the trail loops back through some native grasses before it takes a sharp turn to the right. At about 0.25 mile there is a bench on the left of the trail from which you can relax and look out over the bay.

Next along the trail you pass through some coastal scrub and head up a small hill where you will see a good view of the San Francisco skyline across Richardson Bay.

The bird life here is abundant and varied, so be sure to bring binoculars. Children can learn about some of the differences between how water birds and land birds live. Look for where the small land birds live and try to determine what they eat. Compare that with where the water birds live and what they eat.

Continue on the trail past the Lyford House, a lovingly restored Victorian mansion, and a thicket of impenetrable scrub that is home to hundreds of small birds, and on to the footbridge leading to the education center.

This Victorian houses a great visitor center.

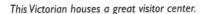

89 RODEO LAGOON TRAIL LOOP

Type ■ Day hike
Difficulty ■ Easy for children
Distance ■ 1.5-mile loop
Hiking time ■ 1 hour
Elevation gain ■ Minimal
Hikable ■ Year-round
Map ■ Rambler's Guide to Trails of Mount
Tamalpais and the Marin Headlands,
Olmsted & Brothers

This is an excellent hike for those just beginning nature hikes with young children, or for those who wish a good introduction to the natural history of the Marin Headlands. Rodeo Lagoon in the Golden Gate National Recreational Area is a natural lagoon formed by beach buildup. It generally catches fresh water that flows down the valley from ridges above, but waves occasionally wash over the beach during winter storms, forming brackish water.

Take the Conzelman Road exit just north of the Golden Gate

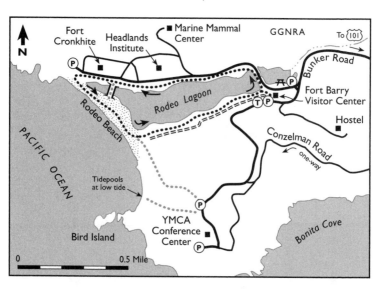

Rodeo Lagoon and Beach make a great outing close to the city.

Bridge and continue for about 1 mile. Turn right on McCullough Road for less than a mile, then turn left on Bunker Road and continue for 2 miles to the parking area.

Rodeo Beach is often a surprise for first-time visitors because it is covered with tiny, multicolored pebbles. These are primarily chert and greenstone. The reddish chert is a hard mineral that does not break down into sand particles, and a barrier of this gravel extends about 1500 feet out into the ocean from the beach and protects the beach from strong wave action.

In addition to chert and greenstone, those interested in rocks can find jasper, carnelian, agate, and other semiprecious stones along the beach. Park rules prohibit collecting, so just look, don't take. Children love to play with the many small pebbles on the beach. Have them see how many different colored pebbles they can find, and see if anyone can find one of the rare carnelians, which are a deep orange-red, unlike any other pebble found here. (The beach was once named Carnelian Beach.)

You can start the Rodeo Lagoon Trail Loop at the picnic area or the visitor center. It circles the lagoon and also follows a section of the beach. A footbridge crosses a creek at the end of the lagoon away from the ocean, by the picnic area.

Rodeo Lagoon, which is about 0.5 mile long and 0.25 mile wide, is an important stop on the migration routes of many birds; hence, bird watching is popular here. Canvasback, bufflehead, and merganser ducks can be seen in large numbers during fall and winter. Brown pelicans and cormorants are plentiful during the summer months, when they can be seen in one of their favorite resting spots, Bird Island, offshore from the lagoon.

Guided walks are led from the visitor center, and the displays there help you learn about the natural history of the area. The California

Marine Mammal Center, a nonprofit facility licensed to rescue and rehabilitate sick or injured marine mammals, is located near the Headlands Institute and offers visitors a chance to view some of the animals being rehabilitated, as well as an occasional tour of the facility.

90 COAST TRAIL TO SLACKER HILL

Type ▪	Day hike
Difficulty ▪	Moderate to difficult for children
Distance ▪	4 miles, round trip
Hiking time ▪	2 to 3 hours
Elevation gain ▪	600 feet
Hikable ▪	Year-round
Map ▪	Rambler's Guide to Trails of Mount Tamalpais and the Marin Headlands, Olmsted & Brothers

This section of the Coast Trail, which is also an integral link in the 400-mile-long Bay Ridge, is about two-thirds complete. The trail offers panoramic views of San Francisco Bay, Alcatraz Island, the San Francisco skyline, Rodeo Lagoon, and the open ocean. On a clear day, the Farallon Islands are visible from the top of Slacker Hill. The trail leads up the east side of the ridge and passes through open grassland and low scrub. Thirty-five different wildflowers have been identified along the trail, and birds are plentiful during breeding times. A special feature of the trail is that it leads through a narrow funnel in the West Coast migration route of raptors. Raptors are large birds that seize their prey by diving down from the sky. They include hawks, owls, and eagles.

The trail begins from a large parking lot on the west side of US 101 at the north end of the Golden Gate Bridge. This lot is across the freeway from the more popular Vista Point parking lot and can be reached by taking the Alexander Avenue exit when heading north. Double back under the freeway at the first left turn and go up Conzelman Road. A short way uphill, turn left into the parking lot. If you're going south on US 101, take the Conzelman Road exit and turn left into the lot.

Broad wooden steps at the trailhead lead from the parking lot into a cypress grove. As you leave the trees, the trail takes a wide turn uphill, and at 0.25 mile crosses Conzelman Road. Crosswalk lines indicate the direction of the trail. As you climb, the sounds of automobiles on the bridge and freeway slowly diminish, and you enter into a world of raptors, grassland, and monarch butterflies, who stop over on the low bushes on the hillsides during their fall migration south.

The panorama from the trail includes all of the bay to the east and the rainbow entrance to Waldo Tunnel to the north. Outcroppings of sedimentary rocks show signs of folding and uplifting near the tunnel.

At about 0.75 mile you come to a spring that seeps out of the hillside above the trail and a short bridge that leads over a small creek. The water attracts a variety of birds and animals, and the surrounding growth supports many nesting birds during breeding season. Deer, bobcat, coyote, and badger signs are frequently evident along this section of the trail.

A little past 1 mile, you come to another seep, a bridge over a larger creek that runs most of the year (all year in wet times) and plenty of bracken ferns, sawgrass, alder, and willow. Again, signs of wildlife are plentiful. At both springs you can rest and enjoy the interesting views or stop and search for signs of the animals that come for water. Raccoons leave tracks about 2 inches long that look like small hands. Deer tracks look like half an oval divided in two parts, and bobcat tracks look like large house cat tracks. Scat, or feces, of these animals is also frequently found near the springs. Try to guess what animal left the scat if you find any. Does it look like that of a cat? If it does, it might

Kids love this entrance to the Coast Trail.

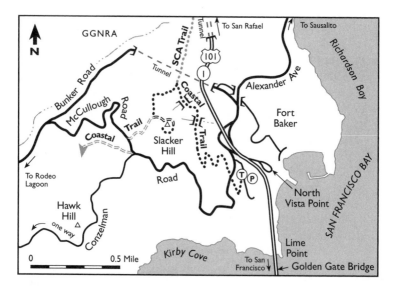

have been from a bobcat. If it looks like that of a dog, it was probably from a coyote. The trail is mostly uphill to the first spring, but levels out for a short stretch before heading back up after the second spring. It reaches a saddle at about 1.25 miles where it intersects with the SCA Trail. This is a good turnaround point if anyone in the party is tired, but most will want to turn left toward Rodeo Lagoon. Mountain bikes are allowed on this trail; watch and listen for them as you go around corners.

At about 1.5 miles you reach the top of the ridge and can see Rodeo Lagoon in the distance, as well as much of the Marin Headlands. At this point you enter a hawk migration study area, and the scientists conducting the study ask that you not linger long or leave the trail in the study area between August 15 and December 15. The trail leads through the highest concentration of migrating raptors in the West, and you will be tempted to stand and observe these birds of prey as they skim the tops of the ridges around you.

About 200 yards downhill from the study area an old road leads uphill to the left. This road circles the study area to the south and ends at the top of Slacker Hill, which is an excellent picnic area, with a large flat area providing a 360-degree view of San Francisco, the bay, and Marin, but it can be cold and windy. Hawks are also easily spotted here, even after the migration season has ended.

You return by the same trails.

INDEX

ABOUT THE AUTHORS

After almost twenty years as a freelance writer, Bill McMillon recently returned to the classroom, where he is teaching environmental and Earth sciences to sometimes-enthused high school students. Bill has explored the outdoors since his childhood days in Mississippi, and his son Kevin has continued this family tradition. Nowadays most of Kevin's explorations are on a snowboard in the Colorado Rockies. He finds time for classes at the University of Colorado in between his snowboarding trips.

THE MOUNTAINEERS, founded in 1906, is a nonprofit outdoor activity and conservation club, whose mission is "to explore, study, preserve, and enjoy the natural beauty of the outdoors . . . ." Based in Seattle, Washington, the club is now the third-largest such organization in the United States, with 15,000 members and five branches throughout Washington State.

The Mountaineers sponsors both classes and year-round outdoor activities in the Pacific Northwest, which include hiking, mountain climbing, ski-touring, snowshoeing, bicycling, camping, kayaking and canoeing, nature study, sailing, and adventure travel. The club's conservation division supports environmental causes through educational activities, sponsoring legislation, and presenting informational programs. All club activities are led by skilled, experienced volunteers, who are dedicated to promoting safe and responsible enjoyment and preservation of the outdoors.

If you would like to participate in these organized outdoor activities or the club's programs, consider a membership in The Mountaineers. For information and an application, write or call The Mountaineers, Club Headquarters, 300 Third Avenue West, Seattle, WA 98119; 206-284-6310.

The Mountaineers Books, an active, nonprofit publishing program of the club, produces guidebooks, instructional texts, historical works, natural history guides, and works on environmental conservation. All books produced by The Mountaineers Books fulfill the club's mission.

Send or call for our catalog of more than 500 outdoor titles:

The Mountaineers Books
1001 SW Klickitat Way, Suite 201
Seattle, WA 98134
800-553-4453
mbooks@mountaineersbooks.org
www.mountaineersbooks.org

The Mountaineers Books is proud to be a corporate sponsor of Leave No Trace, whose mission is to promote and inspire responsible outdoor recreation through education, research, and partnerships. The Leave No Trace program is focused specifically on human-powered (nonmotorized) recreation.

Leave No Trace strives to educate visitors about the nature of their recreational impacts, as well as offer techniques to prevent and minimize such impacts. Leave No Trace is best understood as an educational and ethical program, not as a set of rules and regulations.

For more information, visit *www.LNT.org*, or call 800-332-4100.